Literacy in Action

AUTHORS

Arnold Toutant
Sharon Jeroski
Jean Bowman
Rick Chambers
Richard Davies
Susan Doyle
Kathleen Gregory
Raymond Lavery
Tamar Stein
Dirk Verhulst
Jerry Wowk

PEARSON
Education Canada

GRADE 7 PROJECT TEAM

Team Leader: Anita Borovilos
Publishers: Susan Green, Elynor Kagan
Research and Communications Manager: Paula Smith
Managing Editors: Caroline Kloss, Monica Schwalbe
Developmental Editor: Cathy Fraccaro
Production Editor: Marie Kocher
Production Coordinator: Sharlene Ross
Senior Manufacturing Coordinator: Jane Schell
Art Director: Zena Denchik
Designers: Zena Denchik, Word & Image Design
Permissions Research: Nadia Chapin
Photo Research: Mary Rose MacLachlan
Vice-President Publishing and Marketing: Mark Cobham

ISBN-13: 978-0-13-205903-9
ISBN-10: 0-13-205903-7

Printed and bound in Canada.
1 2 3 4 5 TC 12 11 10 09 08

The publisher has taken every care to meet or exceed industry specifications for the manufacture of textbooks. The cover of this sewn book is a premium, polymer-reinforced material designed to provide long life and withstand rugged use. Mylar gloss lamination has been applied for further durability.

CONSULTANTS

Andrea Bishop
Faye Brownlie
Caren Cameron
Maria Carty
Robert Cloney
Catherine Costello
Christine Finochio
Pat Horstead
Don Jones
Sherri Robb

SPECIALIST REVIEWERS

Aboriginal: Sheila Staats
Equity: Yaw Obeng
Levelling: Barbara Boate
Deborah Kekewich
Science: Catherine Little
Social Studies: Adolfo Diiorio
Special Education: Connie Warrender

ADVISORS AND REVIEWERS

Noreen Blake (Brampton, ON)
Jennifer Brace (Milton, ON)
Connie Bray (London, ON)
Nancy Burdeniuk (Sudbury, ON)
James Cain (Dundas, ON)
Nadine Cormack (Churchill, ON)
Kathyrn D'Angelo (Richmond, BC)
Ann Donaldson (Kanata, ON)
Pat Dooley (Nelson, BC)
Gloria Gustafson (Port Coquitlam, BC)
James Hansen (Victoria, BC)
Brian Harrison (Keswick, ON)
Douglas Hilker (Toronto, ON)
Sharon Horner (North Vancouver, BC)
Meredyth Kezar (Vancouver, BC)
Vickie Morgado (Mississauga, ON)
Nadine Naughton (Victoria, BC)
Maureen Peats (Waterloo, ON)
Bruno Pullara (Woodbridge, ON)
Tammy Renyard (Victoria, BC)
Barb Rushton (New Minas, NS)
Rey Sandre (Etobicoke, ON)
Nanci-Jane Simpson (Hamilton, ON)
Kim Smith (Newmarket, ON)
Lori Spadafora (St. Catherines, ON)
Glenn Thistle (Brantford, ON)
Max Vecchiarino (Mississauga, ON)
Raymond Wiersma (London, ON)
Marian Wilson (London, ON)

STUDENT ADVISORS

Rebecca Barrett
Kaitlyn Bell
Hazel Ann Bowhay
Bryan Cathcart
Matthew Eisen
Luke Fraccaro
Mark Fraccaro
Keith Fukakusa
Kodie Hillaire
Jordan Kovacs
Rebecca Lum
Danielle Mallozzi
Nicholas Renyard
Anton Rodrigo
Leah Rose
Kevin Seemungal
Alex Warrender
Kate Warrender
Amy Yang

HIGHLIGHTS

In this book, you will be learning about how our actions affect the natural world. *EcoZone* gives you lots of opportunities to work with the whole class, with other students, and on your own.

EXPLORE IDEAS
Talk about environmental issues.

EXPLORE RECOUNTS
Practise reading and writing recounts.

EXPLORE GENRES
Compare different genres.

SPOTLIGHT ON LEARNING
Learn about recounts and show what you know.

Contents

EcoZone

EXPLORE IDEAS

EXPLORE RECOUNTS

EXPLORE GENRES

SPOTLIGHT ON LEARNING

How do our actions affect the natural world?

In this unit, you can...

- discuss, read, and view how human actions affect the natural world.
- apply comprehension strategies when you read recounts and view photos.

- write a recount on an environmental issue.
- analyze news media to identify perspective.

At the end of the unit, you can use what you know to create a public service announcement.

Earth Alert!

Get Ready

- Make connections. What environmental issues do the photographs show?
- View with a purpose. Photographers want to share images that have a powerful impact. Which image has the most impact on you?

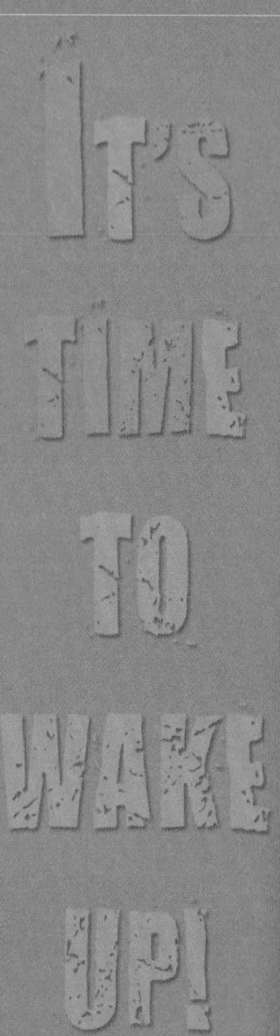

IT'S TIME TO ACT!

NOW!

Sound off

1. Talk to a partner about the environmental issues shown in this collection of photographs.
2. Talk with a group. What environmental issue concerns you the most? Imagine you are a team hired to create an advertising campaign about your issue. In your team meeting, brainstorm the best ways to bring your issue to the public's attention.

When speaking...

Use an expressive voice to emphasize key ideas.

Make sure everyone's ideas are included.

Use specific examples.

Use precise vocabulary.

When listening...

Ask questions to get more information.

Visualize to make sense of the information.

Show interest in the ideas of others.

Reading Recounts

An informational recount tells about the observations and experiences of the writer. Look at the diary below and think about how you might read it.

If you want to visualize what the author is saying, ask...
- What images does the title create in my mind?
- What pictures come to mind about the people, setting, and events?
- What other images do the photographs trigger?

Bering Sea Expedition Diary

by Margaret Williams

Melting ice floes make it harder for polar bears to hunt for food, since they use the floes to get close to their prey, the seal.

Part 5: On the ice

It's thrilling to be on the ice, learning about it from the people who live with and on it all of their lives. The ice is also the most important habitat for the polar bear. All year long I've been reading the latest scientific reports and looking at satellite images from scientists, describing the climate-related changes in ice cover. But the issue becomes more real and urgent as I stand on the ice and hear stories from our native colleagues who are experiencing climate change first hand. Vlad and Sergey explain that the ice edge now recedes earlier in the spring and is forming, on average, three weeks later in the autumn, thereby shortening the season of ice for wildlife and people whose livelihoods and cultures are so closely linked with this ecosystem.

If you want to make sure you understand what you are reading, pause and check. Ask...
- What did I learn?
- Does that make sense?
- How does this information connect to what I read before?

Interpret Photographs

Photographs can provide information that isn't included in the text and can help the reader visualize the people, setting, and events. **When you interpret a photograph...**

- Scan the whole photograph.
- Focus on the main feature (focal point).
- Examine the details around the focal point.
- Read the caption.
- Think about how the photograph makes you feel.
- Consider the photographer's purpose

Melting ice floes make it harder for polar bears to hunt for food, since they use the floes to get close to their prey, the seal.

Summarize in a Graphic Organizer

A web is a useful organizer to **summarize** or generate observations.

REFLECT ON READING

Which strategies will be most helpful to use when you read personal recounts?

Destination Vanuatu

Port Vila **Eretoka Island**

May 5, Port Vila

After spending 36 hours staring at the grey walls of airports and airplanes, my first view of Vanuatu brought only one word to mind: paradise. That's the best word to describe the turquoise water, dazzling sunshine, white sand, and towering palm trees.

A Tiny Corner of Paradise

Visiting this tiny island country is a dream come true. Vanuatu is a string of islands that stretches out in the South Pacific, between Fiji and Australia. Many of the islands are former volcanoes. It has a population of about 200,000. The Ni-Vanuatu (as the people call themselves) live a very simple, village-based life. It is about as different from the urban life in Canada as you can find.

For a diver like me, Vanuatu is a dream destination because of its remarkable ocean life. I'm here to volunteer as a coral reef monitor. I'll be part of a group of divers and environmentalists who've signed up to collect data about the health of Vanuatu's coral reefs. Environmental groups and scientists will then be able to help us understand how we can best protect the coral reefs.

APPLY STRATEGIES

- Visualize.
- Pause and check.
- Interpret the photographs.
- Summarize.

by Susan Doyle

Malekula Island Epi Island Uri Island

Joseph, our Ni-Vanuatu trainer and guide, has been teaching us about coral reefs. I've learned that coral reefs...

- are one of the planet's most important **ecosystems**; along with tropical rainforests, they are the most important source of biological diversity.
- are home to a quarter of all fish species.
- provide 10 percent of the world's food.
- protect coastlines around the world.

That's the good news. The bad news is that 10 percent of the world's coral reefs are already gone and almost 60 percent are threatened.

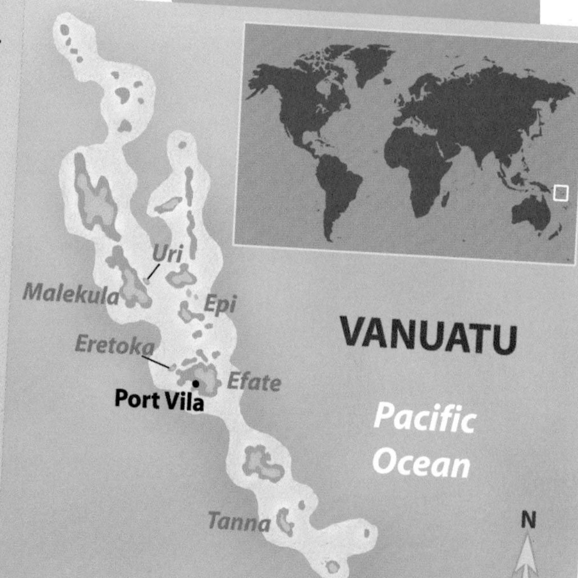

Here are some of the threats:

- volcanic eruptions, hurricanes, and earthquakes
- overfishing
- growth of human settlements
- global warming
- pollution from chemicals and industries

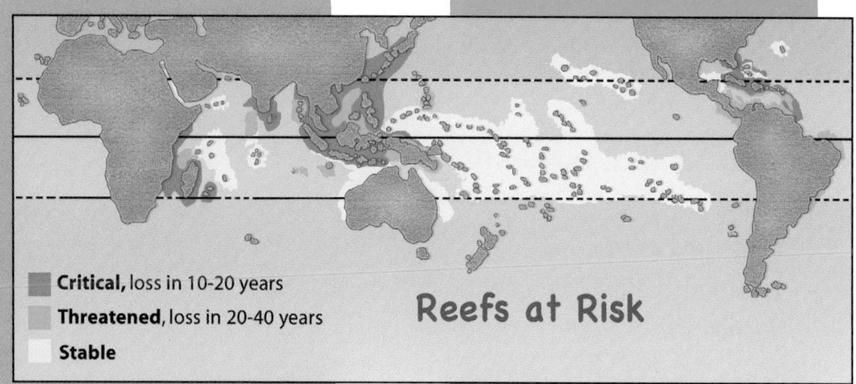

That's where we come in. Our information might help scientists find answers to the really important questions about coral reefs: What threats do they face? And, what can be done to protect them?

So friends, I'm going diving. And don't worry, I'm practising my mantra: "Take only photos; leave only bubbles." Stay tuned.

ecosystem a place on Earth where living things interact with other living and non-living things

Day 4

Port Vila

Eretoka Island

May 8, Eretoka Island

Just as we arrived at the Port Vila harbour this morning, the skies opened in a tropical downpour. While we scrambled to find shelter, we noticed several women in the nearby marketplace calmly reaching for banana leaves. They casually held them over their heads. Hard to beat that for a "green" solution—a biodegradable umbrella!

The Coral Reef Ecosystem

From the harbour, we headed for Eretoka Island, a tiny island fringed by reefs. We spent the day diving and counting fish. This gave us a first-hand view of how a healthy coral reef ecosystem works.

First, we sailed along the edge of a mangrove swamp that seemed to go on forever.

Mangrove trees are unusual because their roots grow in saltwater instead of soil. The huge tangle of vegetation and roots creates excellent breeding grounds for birds and coral reef marine life. Mangroves are a major source of food and habitat for young ocean creatures. Mangroves also **stabilize** the shoreline. This, in turn, reduces erosion. Coastal erosion is a major problem for reefs. When **silt** blocks out the sun, it is hard for the coral to survive.

APPLY STRATEGIES

- Visualize.
- Pause and check.
- Interpret the photographs.
- Summarize.

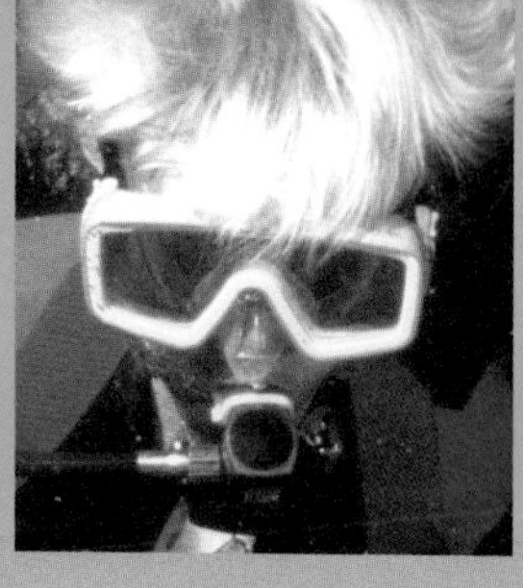

Malekula Island Epi Island Uri Island

Joseph explained that for most people, mangroves are just big muddy swamps. When developers want to build along the coast, the mangroves are the first thing to go. What people don't understand is that rich coral gardens and swampy mangroves go hand in hand.

Next, we discovered the role that seagrasses play in keeping coral reefs healthy. These flowering marine plants provide food and habitat for sea-dwelling animals. Turtles, manatees, fish, sea urchins, and Vanuatu's best known (if ugliest) sea creature, the sea cucumber, can be found in the seagrasses. Like mangroves, seagrasses provide breeding grounds for sealife. They also help filter **sediment** from the water. They stabilize the sea bottom and prevent coastal erosion.

You can see the roots in this mangrove swamp.

Seagrass

We paddled our kayaks back to our sailboat and got set to do our reef monitoring. Schools of fish filled an underwater landscape that looked like a movie set. There were plunging cliffs, huge caves, and a maze of underwater tunnels formed by frozen lava. And there was coral everywhere!

The best moment of all, though I didn't think it at the time, was seeing a white-tip reef shark. Only days ago, I would have wanted to see that shark dead. But I've learned that sharks are becoming one of the most endangered sea creatures. Now that I see how everything has its place in this ecosystem, I'd like to think that sharks will survive—and actually thrive.

A sea cucumber

stabilize to make firm or steady

silt fine sand, clay, or other soil

sediment silt, sand, mud, and gravel carried by water

Day 7

Port Vila

Eretoka Island

May 11, Malekula Island

We got a surprise wake-up, or maybe shakeup, early this morning. We were jolted awake by a small earthquake. I watched my books and camera gear bounce across the desk. I wondered if I should dive under the desk in case the shaking got worse. Lucky for us, the only damage was to our sleep.

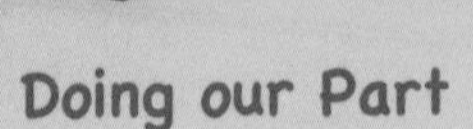

Doing our Part

Just yesterday, Joseph told us that Vanuatu is on the edge of the "Ring of Fire." This is a chain of volcanoes that encircles the Pacific Ocean. Every few months, Vanuatu rocks and rolls from earthquakes and volcanic explosions. It even has an active volcano on the island of Tanna.

Our dive today was in an area that was hit by a strong earthquake 40 years ago. The jolt lifted the edge of the tiny island of Uri. It destroyed the shoreline, the mangrove swamps, the seagrass beds, and the reef beyond. Even though the changes were natural, they upset the whole coral reef ecosystem.

One of the worst threats to the reefs is the crown-of-thorns starfish. It survives by sucking the guts out of living coral. It can be as big as 80 cm across and have as many as 21 arms. Even scarier, it is covered in really sharp, venomous spines. So, our mission today was to hunt, capture, and then destroy them.

APPLY STRATEGIES

- Visualize.
- Pause and check.
- Interpret the photographs.
- Summarize.

I found it hard to hate something that has been living on these reefs for thousands of years. It's not as if they have anywhere else to go. The problem is that they eat coral. The more starfish there are, the more the coral gets eaten. Over the past 50 years or so, they have spread to all parts of the Pacific. In places where their numbers are high, they can kill all of the coral, leaving only dead skeletons.

A crown-of-thorns starfish feeds on coral.

So, if the crown-of-thorns starfish has been around for so long, why is it suddenly such a threat? Scientists aren't really sure. They think it is due to several changes happening at once. New building along the shoreline destroys mangrove and seagrass areas. Overfishing reduces the number of predator fish. Volcanic eruptions, like the one that hit Uri, cover coral reefs in sand and debris. This blocks the sunlight that the coral needs to survive.

Or maybe it is the disappearance of tritons. These are large sea snails with very beautiful shells. They can be found for sale in markets all over the Pacific. Sadly, they are also the major predator of the crown-of-thorns starfish. Could the starfish be **flourishing** simply because tritons are being sold as souvenirs?

Well, we tried to do our part. We captured 21 of the starfish. We took them back to shore to burn them. I felt bad about throwing them in the fire. It turns out that even broken pieces of the starfish can **regenerate**. So, we decided to help save the Uri reef—we wouldn't take any chances.

A triton feeds on a crown-of-thorns starfish.

flourishing thriving or doing well

regenerate to regrow

Day 8

Port Vila **Eretoka Island**

May 12, Epi Island

Today we took a break from diving to explore a traditional village on the island of Epi. We arrived by boat and were welcomed by the locals who led us into their village. The chief took us to a palm-thatched hut. This is where we would be spending the night. Our beds were colourful woven mats, spread out on a well-swept dirt floor.

APPLY STRATEGIES

- Visualize.
- Pause and check.
- Interpret the photographs.
- Summarize.

Treading Lightly on Earth

The village is small by Canadian standards. About 200 people live in little groups of thatched huts. Taro and other roots, which are the basis of the traditional diet, are grown just beyond these houses. We walked by carefully tended plots of cabbage and other local greens. Banana, mango, and papaya trees surrounded the gardens. In a clearing between the huts, women used banana, palm, and pandanus leaves to weave baskets and mats.

As we were touring the village, we spotted several **outrigger** canoes on the beach. Before we knew it, we were out on the turquoise waves, heading for a nearby reef. The outrigger is a marvel of technology. It is the main form of transportation on many tropical islands.

It's fast, light, built with local materials, and virtually free. It's hard to imagine a better boat!

Our first thrill was seeing a school of flying fish. Their silver fins flashed as they dipped below the waves and then emerged into the sun. They looked like a flock of birds. I threw on my snorkel and mask, and dived off the side of the outrigger. Too late, I saw the turtles swimming right below me. I didn't seem to bother them, though.

Another joy was swimming with a dugong. This giant, gentle mammal allowed us to swim right up to her and even rub her side. The dugong is endangered in much of the world, mainly due to the disappearance of seagrass. As we watched, the dugong kept diving down to the ocean floor to graze on seagrass.

A villager steers an outrigger canoe.

A flying fish

As we headed back to shore late in the afternoon, we saw the village from a distance. It looked timeless and idyllic. It made me think about how the Ni-Vanuatu have lived this simple life for thousands of years, taking just enough from the environment to survive. I've heard environmentalists talk about treading lightly on the earth—well, now I've seen the real thing.

A dugong

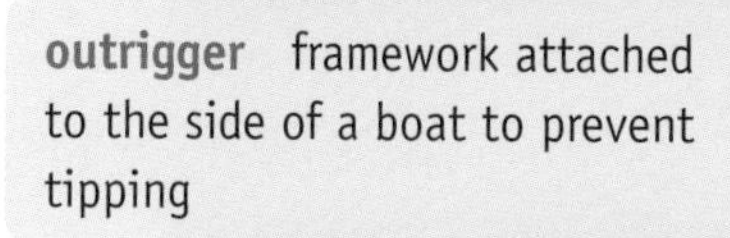

outrigger framework attached to the side of a boat to prevent tipping

Day 10

Port Vila　　Eretoka Island

May 14, Uri Island

Today's trip was my last in Vanuatu. We were lucky that the chief and two environmentalists were with us. They had agreed to show us the work they were doing to protect the coral reefs. I really wanted to learn what the future of these reefs would be.

APPLY STRATEGIES

- Visualize
- Pause and check.
- Interpret the photographs.
- Summarize.

A Valuable Life Lesson

Our first stop was Uri, a tiny island off the coast of Malekula. Fifteen years ago, the village chief made some reef areas "tabu" (in English, taboo). If a chief says something is tabu, it means he has placed a restriction on it. All the people must respect this. In this case, it meant the reef area was protected. No one can go there or take anything from it.

It didn't take our team long to see that the tabu was working. On our first dive, we counted a great number of large fish. A huge green humphead parrotfish swam past me. He looked like a security guard watching the reef. We spotted triggerfish and other fish that like to eat the crown-of-thorns starfish. No wonder there was no sign of them here.

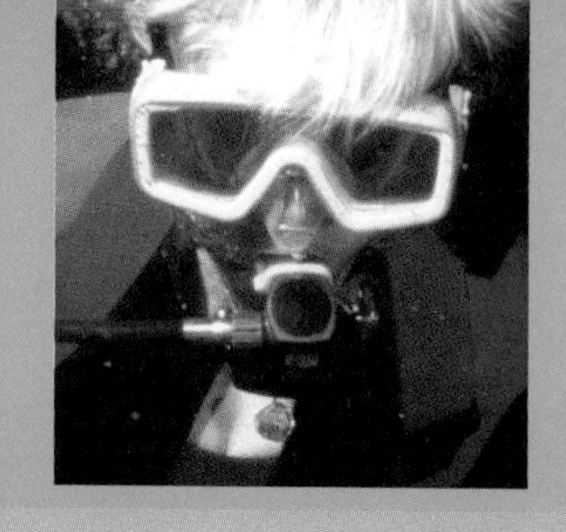

Our next dive was at another protected area off Malekula. Once again, we saw many fish like snappers and groupers. This was good to see because these species were often overfished for their commercial value. My thrill for the day was spotting a moustache or titan triggerfish. Wow!

Finally, we landed on a reef-fringed island. Here, a group of chiefs had worked together to protect the reef. They put a **ban** on net fishing and night spearfishing (using light to attract fish) during the breeding season. The ban helped stop overfishing in the reef ecosystem. The new bans have the support of the local people. They depend on the reef and want to keep it healthy.

My brush with a humphead parrot fish

A moustache or titan triggerfish

Bleached coral

Joseph reminded us of the coral bleaching in the Indian Ocean that seemed to be caused by global warming. This loss of colour in a coral reef was a sign of stress. He told us that so far, their reefs were OK. The slight rise in the ocean temperature hadn't caused much bleaching yet. But it could still happen. It is one of the most important reasons for protecting the reefs now. The healthier the reefs are, the more chance they have to recover if there is a bleaching event.

As we said goodbye to the chiefs, I asked them what they hoped the future would hold for their precious coral reefs. One chief spoke up quickly in his own language, and Joseph translated just as quickly. "Everything around us is our place. If we take care of it, it will take care of us." Sounds like a lesson for all of us.

ban an order to stop

Looking *for* Seabirds

Get Ready

- Predict. Preview the text features (headings, illustrations, map) to predict what Sophie Webb's journal is about.
- Pause and check. After each dated journal entry, pause and think about what ideas are facts and what ideas are opinions.

by Sophie Webb

Seabirds have always fascinated me. A diverse group, they spend the majority of their lives at sea, returning to land only to breed and perhaps occasionally to roost. One way I study seabirds is by observation, however, trying to study creatures that live on and in the deep ocean is difficult. How to see them?

Fortunately, I have been able to work on several different research vessels as an observer, censusing, or counting, seabirds. I have been on cruises to the Arctic, the tip of South America, and the Antarctic. Some have been a couple weeks long, others a month or two. Now I am off to work for a month as a seabird observer for Dr. George Hunt along the Aleutian Island chain, in Alaska.

Red-footed Booby from the tropics

16 May

The day dawns absolutely beautiful: sunny, clear, and calm. After a delay, the engines start their rumbling to warm up, then their roar, and we leave Seward by 10:00 A.M. We travel 15 to 20 kilometres off the coast.

The main purpose of this cruise is to investigate possible causes of the population decline of the Steller's sea lion. We are trying to discover whether this decline is due to killer whale **predation** or lack of available food. We also want to know where in the Aleutians there is an abundance of food and what causes this abundance. The project then has several components that will help us understand the Aleutian Island system better: oceanography, marine biology, **mammalogy**, and **ornithology**. My job falls under ornithology: I study seabirds. Seabirds can be indicators of the availability of food to animals that feed high on the food chain, like Steller's sea lions.

So why is it important to understand bird distribution in the ocean? Seabirds could help warn us about a change in the health of the ocean. Imagine if a bird population dropped drastically in a certain area; it could indicate that there is a severe decline in the productivity, or food supply, in the ocean for some reason. An El Niño event (a natural warming of the Pacific Ocean that can be mild or drastic depending on the year) might have occurred, or an oil spill, or some other less detectable pollutant might have been introduced into the ocean. Seabirds are very sensitive to these changes, particularly during the breeding season, when they require great amounts of food to feed their growing chicks.

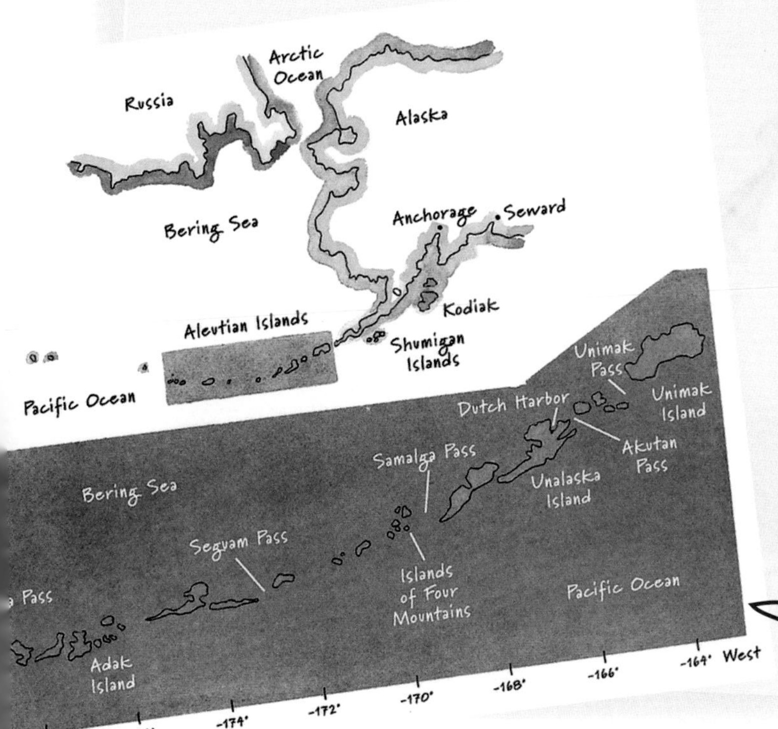

The area of our cruise through the Aleutian Islands in Alaska

predation the natural preying of one animal on another animal or organism

mammalogy the study of mammals

ornithology the study of birds

Today there are a few birds about in small groups. The majority are alcids. Alcids include the puffins, murres, murrelets, and auklets. They are one of the main reasons I wanted to go on this research cruise to the Aleutians. Alcids live only in the northern hemisphere and are thought to be the ecological counterpart of the penguins, found in the southern hemisphere.

Alcids are also found along the Pacific coast of Canada and the United States. Although primarily ocean species, many kinds of alcids feed in the area from the coast out to the edge of the continental shelf. Because it is close to land, this zone is susceptible to a number of negative encounters with humans. There is evidence, for example, that the Common Murre population in California has declined because of oil spills, drownings in nets (birds get caught in the nets when diving for fish and drown), and a reduction in the fish they feed their chicks. Perhaps the most difficult challenge in all the world's oceans is their gradual degradation by human pollution, plastic litter, and overfishing.

A large, eight-centimetre plastic lure for catching fish or squid lodged in the rib cage of a Laysan Albatross. It probably caused the albatross to die. I saw this on Laysan Island when I was working on a cruise in the Hawaiian Island chain.

30 May

Seabirds have been on Earth much longer than we have. But with the advent of humans and the huge increase in our population, seabirds face new challenges. On land, the introduction of goats, rabbits, cats, and rats to remote islands has severely affected the birds' breeding populations. On the ocean, plastic has become a hazard for all marine creatures. To seabirds, floating bits of plastic and Styrofoam beads can look like small jellyfish or zooplankton. Plastic lures and floats can look like squid or fish. The seabirds are fooled and they eat them. Because plastic doesn't break down, it will eventually cause blockages in the digestive tract. I am always surprised that even a thousand kilometres from land I see floating Styrofoam cups, plastic buoys, and drifting pieces of nylon fishing net on the ocean.

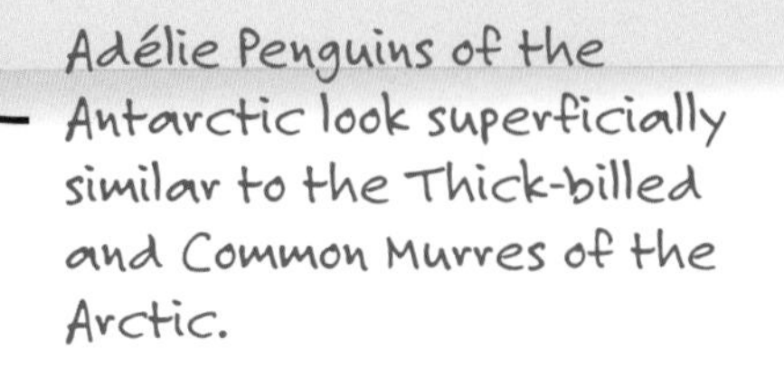

Adélie Penguins of the Antarctic look superficially similar to the Thick-billed and Common Murres of the Arctic.

30 June

On this trip not only have I seen huge numbers of birds, and even a few rare birds, but I've also learned more about the dynamics of the Arctic marine ecosystem. The information that we have gathered will be analyzed and added to a database from previous years. Providing information will help us make wise marine management decisions in the region and will add to the scientific knowledge of the ecosystem.

Every time I go out on the ocean I am reminded of how complex it is—how it is a patchwork of different environments. Also, as time goes on I am made increasingly aware of how fragile the ocean is. It is not limitless, and we humans must be good **stewards** and ensure that the ecosystems remain healthy.

steward a person who attends to the needs of someone or something

React and Respond

1. The author calls the ocean a complex patchwork of environments and says it is not limitless. Explain what you think this means in your own words.
2. A recount often includes facts, opinions, and personal reactions. Find at least two examples of each in the selection.

Build Word Power

3. Whenever you read about science, you are likely to encounter words that end in *–ology*, which means "the science of." Here are some other *–ology* words. Identify the field of science by looking at the first part of these words.
   - climatology
   - glaciology
   - parasitology
   - microbiology

WRITER'S FILE

- Read like a writer. How does the writer let her readers know how much she cares about her topic?
- News reporters try to keep an objective voice in their work. They try to represent all perspectives on a topic. With a partner, use the information in the selection to write a short news report about something that concerns you. Keep your voice objective and present more than one perspective.
- Use ideas from your notes to explain how the author uses her June 30 entry to summarize and persuade readers. What did the author want the reader to think and feel?

Arctic Adventure

by Students on Ice

Arctic Floe Edge Expedition 2006

Between June 15 and 25, a Students on Ice (SOI) group travelled to Pond Inlet on the edge of the frozen Arctic Ocean. The participants were 16 high school students from Canada, the United States, China, and Saudi Arabia, together with a team of scientists, experts, and Inuit guides. During the expedition, participants explored the floe edge region and focused on Arctic flora, fauna, history, science, and culture. With the scientists and Inuit team members, the group also explored the link between Inuit traditional knowledge and sustainable living.

Here are some journal entries written by people on the expedition.

Students on Ice is a Canadian organization that offers unique learning expeditions to the Antarctic and the Arctic. These trips offer a life-changing experience for students from around the world. They learn first-hand the effects of global warming on the polar regions and come home with a new understanding and respect for the planet.

Get Ready

- Make connections. What would you want to experience and learn if you could go on a trip to the Arctic?
- Interpret photographs. Look for information in the photographs before you read.

JUNE 17: EXPEDITION LEADER, GEOFF GREEN

We're very lucky to once again have David Gray with us as a member of our education team. This is David's third SOI expedition to the Arctic. But David has spent many years up in the Arctic since his first visit in 1968. As a research scientist he has been involved with many projects, and he is very well respected for his extensive work and expertise on Arctic animal behaviour, and as a historian.

On this trip, David will be working with the students on several projects: recording the birds species found at the floe edge, especially looking for Ivory Gulls, a species that has always been rare and now is possibly endangered; collecting information on polar bears at the floe edge, including interviews with local hunters and elders; and duplicating sampling of plankton and sea bottom invertebrates for comparison with samples taken in 1955.

Komatiks (sleds) are used to transport everything for the trip to the base camp.

A student reflects on his Arctic experience.

JUNE 19; STUDENT, JONATHAN

Today was our first day at the floe edge. When we arrived at a suitable spot on the edge we started to get settled in. The guides scouted ahead on snowmobiles to search for bears and possibly whales. Little did we expect, five minutes after arriving at the floe edge, one of the guides came zooming back and yelled out, "Whales, whales." Everybody sprinted back to the komatiks and we sped over to the site. After we arrived at the new location, everybody jumped out and started looking toward the open water. Someone yelled out and we saw the beluga whales moving toward us. Then almost instantly, more beluga whales started to pop up from everywhere. I got some good shots and taped a movie of a large group swimming across, about 3 metres from where we were standing. That was amazing. The whales are pure white and are about 5 metres long. They came out and dropped back into the water very gracefully. We saw an estimated 100 beluga whales at that spot in about 10 minutes. One of the biologists on our trip, David, has been travelling to the Arctic for 37 years and has never seen a beluga whale. Our guides have been travelling to that spot for 15 years and never saw a beluga there. I couldn't have asked for more today, as it was one of the rarest days I will ever experience.

The ice camp

Beluga whales

The group celebrates its newly awakened connection to the Arctic.

JUNE 20: STUDENT, JEN

Today was great for lessons on Arctic human history. We stopped by an ancient archaeological site in the morning where the Thule had been. The best part was that we could see artifacts from many time periods, left by the Thule from 1500 years ago, by the Scottish whalers from the 1800s, and by the more recent Inuit. From the Thule, we saw what was left of their homes: huge rocks with remnants of bowhead whale skulls, caribou bones, etc. From the Scottish whalers: everything from huge barrel rings to pieces of glass and metal tins. Our Inuit elder guide, Panuilie, said that when the Inuit came to settle in the area, the scared Thule moved inland. And when the whalers came, they used Inuit people to help hunt whales (almost to extinction). So, it's a really neat web of interactions between all these groups of people that have been here that I couldn't have fully understood without being there and "seeing" their past.

JUNE 21: STUDENT, ROSIE

Today was another inspiring and action-packed day. We began with a trip to a bird colony on the Cape Graham Moore cliffs. What an amazing scene it was there—a prime example of what I'd call "organized chaos." There were thousands of birds (mostly Kittiwake gulls) nesting in every possible niche and on every ledge.

After a delicious lunch, we headed out to the floe edge, and again, an amazing array of Arctic animals came by to pay us a visit. First were the narwhals, gracefully slipping through the water, surfacing to breathe. What a neat sound that is. Seals, murres, icebergs, and beautiful scenery kept me occupied for the rest of the time out at the floe edge. It is interesting to contemplate how much life thrives under the calm grey surface of the Arctic Ocean.

Classroom in the field

Flock of murres

I feel very fortunate that we had the chance last night to speak with Panuilie, the eldest Inuit guide on this trip. We would ask him questions in English, and James, another guide, would translate into Inuktitut. I love listening to them speak in Inuktitut, but I don't think there's much hope for me learning it any time soon! Listening to Panuilie talk about climate change was the first time I had seen the personal side of global warming. We hear a lot about the scientific side of the issue, but not a lot about how the Inuit will be impacted. And, indeed, the threats that climate change pose to their cultural way of life are huge. Panuilie felt that the most important message we students should take home from the Arctic is that climate change is a real thing.

The past few days have really made me begin to think about where I fit into this whole Arctic picture. I feel so fortunate to have the opportunity to experience this place first-hand. With a personal connection to the land comes the motivation and inspiration to help contribute to protecting it. There are so many issues and areas to be explored; lots of food for thought.

Icebergs

An Inuit guide shares his personal observations of climate change with a group participant.

React and Respond

1. Explain why Rosie felt that a personal connection to the land would motivate and inspire people to contribute to its protection.
2. Select one image that you feel represents the most important ideas in this selection. Explain why you think so.

Build Word Power

3. The word oxymoron comes from the Greek *oxy* "sharp" plus *moros* "dull." An oxymoron is a phrase that puts together two words that seem to contradict each other. Use the following words to create your own oxymorons: deafening, accident, tradition, genuine, conflict. Try changing adjectives to nouns or nouns to adjectives to find even more combinations.

WRITER'S FILE

- Read like a writer. How does the last paragraph summarize the impact of the writer's experience?
- Write your own concluding paragraph as a student on the expedition. Include how your experiences have affected your understanding and appreciation for the Arctic.

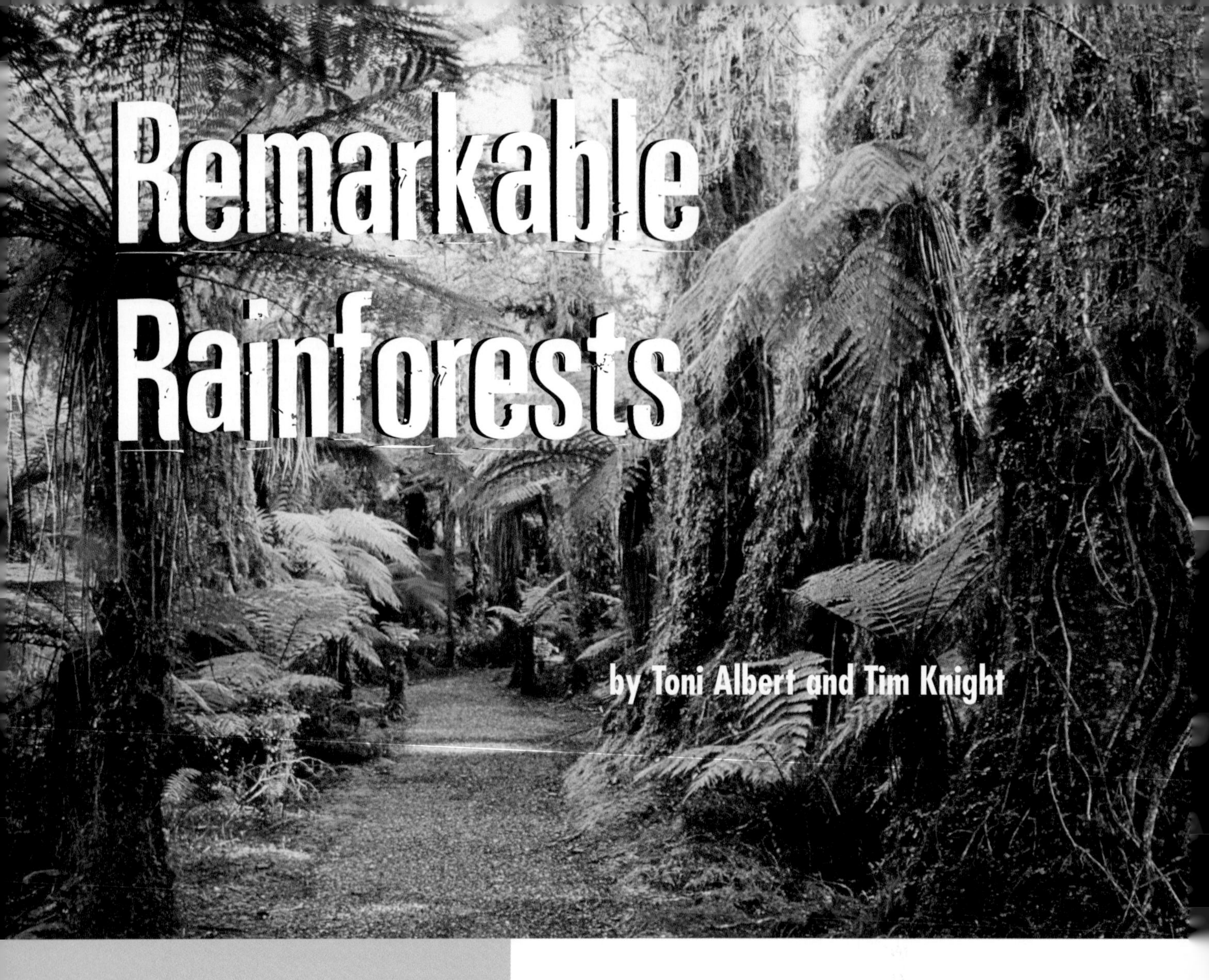

Remarkable Rainforests

by Toni Albert and Tim Knight

Get Ready

Make connections. What do you already know about the topic?

Ask questions. What questions do you have about the world's rainforests?

Earth wears a green belt around its middle, a broad band that stretches out on either side of the equator. There is no winter there. The sun is strong, and the rainfall is measured in metres instead of centimetres. The conditions for life are nearly perfect. No wonder great forests, called rainforests, have developed there.

These ancient forests are powerhouses of life where uncounted species of animals and plants have not even been named. Unfortunately, today many of the world's rainforests are like bombed and blasted cities, where nothing remains but charred black ground. Scientists believe that by the year 2050, there will be no rainforests left to preserve.

Vanishing Rainforests

The map below shows some of the most endangered rainforests in the world and what percentage of rainforest was left in these areas at the beginning of this century.

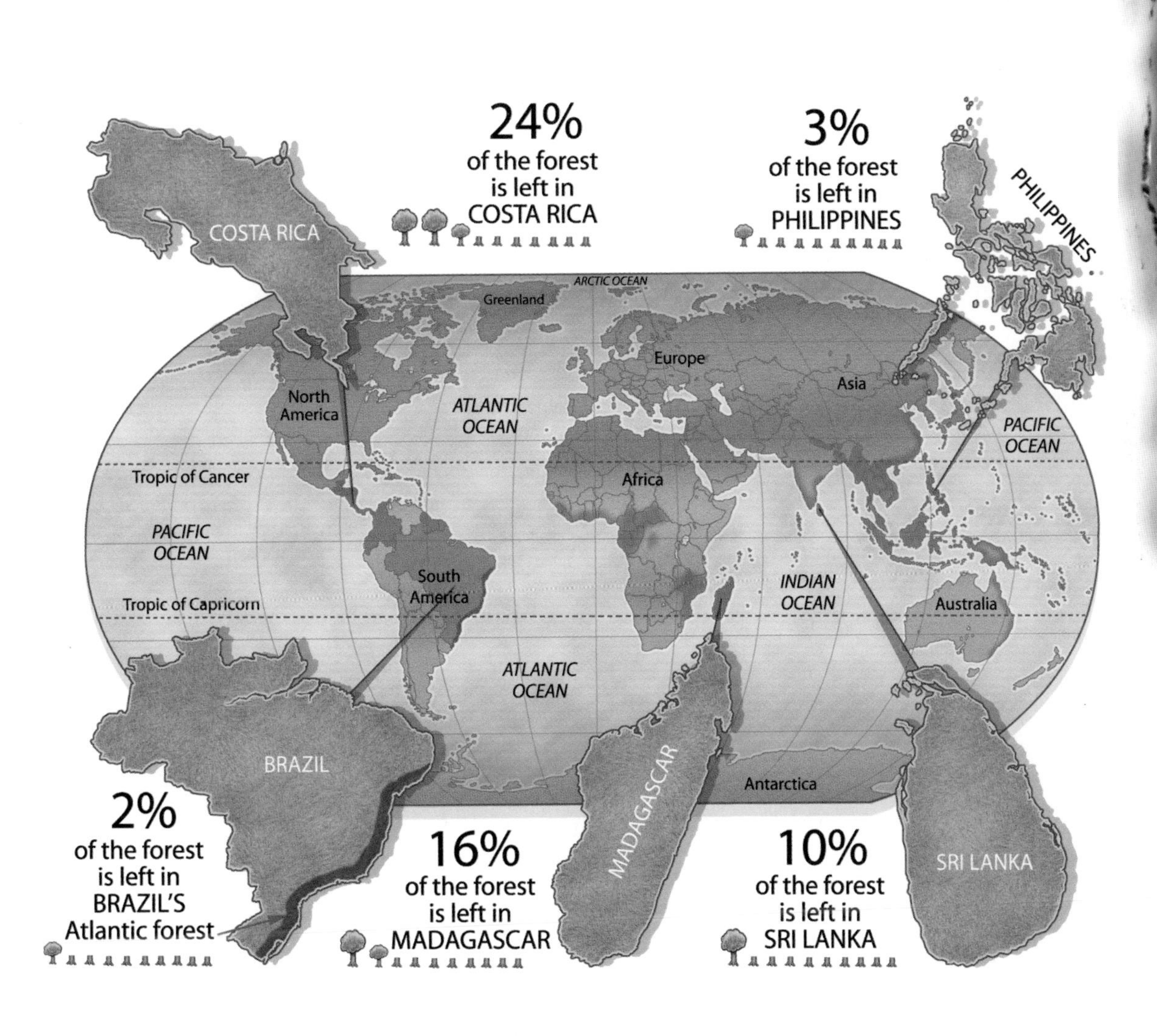

DID YOU KNOW?

Two hundred years ago, rainforests covered 14 percent of all the land in the world. Now they cover less than 4 percent. Almost three quarters of the rainforests on Earth have been destroyed.

Who Destroys the Rainforest?

Since the beginning of this century, almost half of the rainforests in the world have been cut down. Those that are left are being destroyed at the rate of 60 hectares per minute.

Slash-and-burn farming in Indonesia

Poor Farmers

Poor farmers are forced to clear forested land to grow food for their families. Unfortunately, their "slash-and-burn" farming doesn't work when too many people practise it in too small an area. At first, after land is cleared by cutting and burning a section of forest, crops grow well. Nutrients from the ash of the burned forest provide suitable soil for a few years, but soon the soil is worn out. Then, more forest is slashed and burned.

A tea plantation on deforested land

Loggers, Ranchers, and Commercial Farmers

Logging operations cut down the trees in the rainforest to provide wood for construction and industries in other countries, such as Japan and the United States.

Cattle ranchers clear the rainforest to raise beef, which is then sold cheaply for use in fast-food hamburgers and processed meat. Cattle ranching causes serious erosion problems. Within five years, the land is so exhausted that it takes two hectares to support one cow.

Cash crops, such as bananas, coffee, and pineapples, are often grown on huge plantations where there was once rainforest. The fruit is usually exported to Western countries, and some of the plantations are owned by big companies in the United States.

Miners

When valuable iron, oil, or gold is discovered in a rainforest, the forest is cut to make way for the mining operation.

An oil drilling site in the rainforest of Ecuador

Mahogany trees at a lumberyard in Guatemala

Developers and Us

Developers in governments and private businesses clear the rainforests to build roads, dams, towns, and businesses. Some development schemes are unsound. Dams built to provide electricity for the new towns flood thousands of large areas of rainforests. Sometimes, without the forests to prevent erosion, the waterways clog with silt, and the dam doesn't work.

Our demand for rainforest products, such as mahogany furniture, has a lot to do with why rainforests are being cut down. At one time, the demand in North America for fast-food hamburgers supported much of the cattle ranching industry in Central and South America.

The Rainforest Jigsaw Puzzle

Rainforests have existed for millions of years. During that time, plants and animals have filled every available space and worked out the best way to live in their forest home.

After existing side by side for so long, many animals and plants have come to depend on each other for survival. All living things in the rainforest are connected. The system that connects them is known as an ecosystem.

The rainforest ecosystem fits together like a living jigsaw puzzle. If any piece of the puzzle is missing, the whole jigsaw is ruined. When one kind of plant or animal becomes extinct, everything else that depends on it will die too.

Just as one piece of a jigsaw will only fit into one part of the puzzle, every animal and plant has its own special place, known as a habitat. Plants that need bright sunlight cannot live on the dark forest floor. A hungry caterpillar will starve if it strays far from its foodplant. Tadpoles cannot survive without water. The ecosystem is made up of thousands of small habitats. For example, the crown of every tree is like a miniature city, with its own population of permanent residents. Visitors such as monkeys, birds, and insects may come and go, moving from town to town in search of food, but some creatures spend their entire life in the same treetop home. They can never move away, because they rely on the other plants and animals in their neighbourhood.

Fungus is very important. It rots leaf litter quickly, making nutrients for other plants.

Some flowers depend on a particular type of insect to spread their pollen.

React and Respond

1. How do details in the images and on the map help you to understand the ideas in the text?
2. How do the authors try to make their report about the rainforest fair and balanced?

Build Word Power

3. The prefix *eco–* comes from "*oikos*," the Greek word for *house* or *household*. What connection can you make between the original meaning of *eco–* and the meaning it has today in the words *ecosystem*, *ecologist*, and *eco-friendly*?

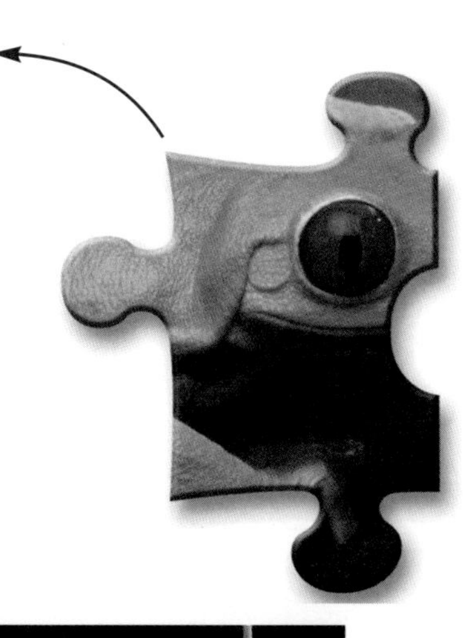

A single tree-top **epiphyte** provides a permanent home for small creatures, such as tree frogs.

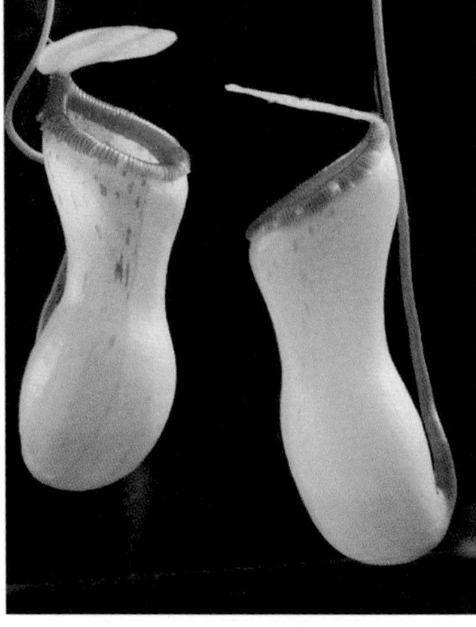

Pitcher plants rely on a diet of insects, without which they could not survive in poor soil.

WRITER'S FILE

- Read like a writer. What do you notice about the writer's choice of vivid language?
- Imagine yourself as an environmentalist visiting a rainforest. Use what you have learned in the selection to write a description of what you observe.

epiphyte a plant that grows on another plant

Writing Recounts

Marcus wrote about his experiences as a volunteer working to preserve a park. Look at his task outline, final draft, and some comments he made about his work.

Topic	*Protecting wildlife*
Purpose	*To inform about an issue*
Audience	*Other students in my class*
Form	*Personal recount*

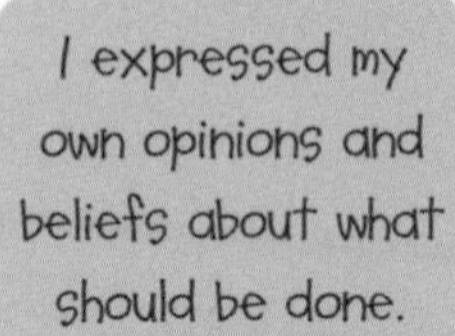

I expressed my own opinions and beliefs about what should be done.

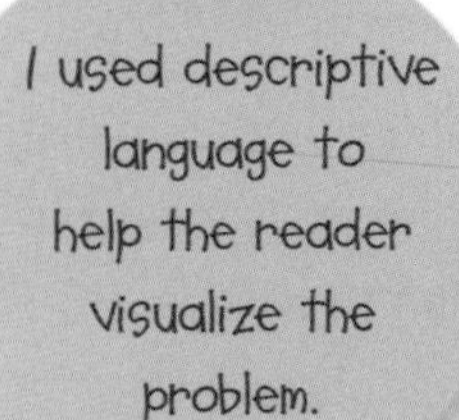

I used descriptive language to help the reader visualize the problem.

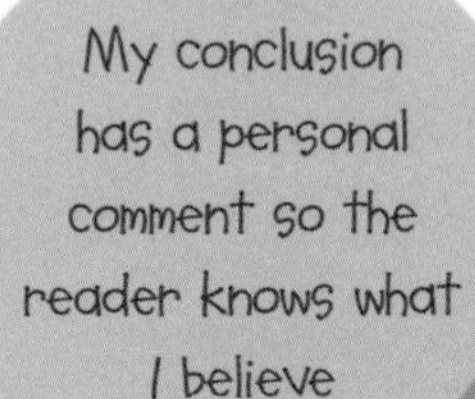

My conclusion has a personal comment so the reader knows what I believe

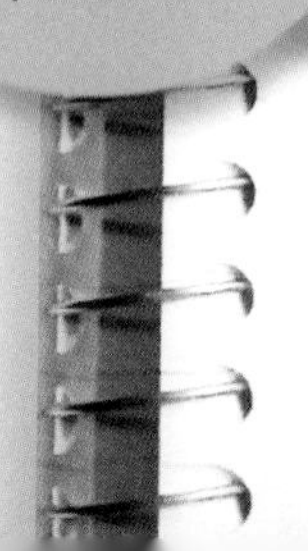

Protecting Boyd Park

My family and I joined a group of volunteers called the Friends of Boyd Park. Boyd Park is in Vaughan, Ontario, and is home to lots of plants and animals. We live right next to the park.

The park was being threatened by developers. There were plans to build a bridge through the park to link a road. We wanted to stop the project because we were worried about noise and car fumes close to our house. We were concerned about wildlife too.

A famous historian also got involved in our protest. He said that building the bridge would open up the area to even *more* development. We also found out that an old Ouendat village site would be affected. The group organized picnics and distributed flyers to raise public awareness.

People listened to our group. The government decided that the bridge would not be built in Boyd Park. The park is now in a protected area.

I believe that the government needs to find ways to cope with our growing population in ways that don't hurt the environment. We have only one planet and we have to protect it.

HINTS

As you plan your writing, ask yourself...

- What language will I use to help readers know I care about the environment?
- How will I group information into paragraphs?
- What images will I include?

Write a Recount

It's your turn to either write about real events that you have experienced, or choose a challenge facing the environment. Then, imagine what it would be like to overcome that challenge.

Ask yourself the following questions:

- What experience or challenge will I write about?
- What will my purpose be?
- Who will read my writing?
- What form will my writing take?

Create a flow chart that will help you plan your recount.

The introduction describes who, what, where, when, why. → The body describes the sequence of events. → The conclusion reflects on the experiences and identifies new questions or next action.

REFLECT ON WRITING

How will you assess your recount? Record three key criteria that will help you. Assess your recount using these criteria.

- What aspect was most successful?
- What aspect will you need to work on?

Guujaaw
An Advocate for the Planet

Imagine that you are a young child born on the Queen Charlotte Islands (now Haida Gwaii) of British Columbia. You spend your youth learning the traditional way of the Haida Nation. You are given your name Guujaaw (meaning "drum") at a formal potlatch ceremony.

Your days are spent living off the land: you dig for clams and pick seaweed with your mother, you fish and hunt with your father, and your uncle teaches you how to set traps. Your great-grandmother, who eventually lives to be 114, teaches you the songs of your people. You learn to drum and dance. The elders of your clan teach you by telling you about their experiences on the land and water. You take journeys around Haida Gwaii by rowboat and canoe, often alone. At 15, you begin carving argillite stone found on Haida Gwaii. Later you study the totems and you learn to carve the cedar. People learn of your skill and ask you to carve special totems and to build canoes and longhouses. Your work is displayed all over the world. You perform in your own country and abroad.

What happens when the way of life you and your people have known is threatened? How do you respond? Your art represents who you and your people are, but now you must also raise your voice to protect the land. You lead protests against logging, mining, offshore oil drilling, and oil tanker traffic.

Get Ready

- Make connections. Think about the word *relationship*. What does "a relationship to Earth" mean to you?
- Find important ideas. As you read, find clues to Guujaaw's perspective on sustainability.

This is the experience of Guujaaw of the Raven Clan, Haida Nation. Guujaaw has been the President of the Haida Nation Council since 2000. He brings the perspective of an artist to his activism and he urges us to develop sustainable ways to use Earth's resources.

"We should be able to live here assured that there will be resources and a life. The problem today is a lot of uncertainty and discomfort from being in a place where we see life being depleted around us and the land getting poorer. It's discouraging to live like that... We have to turn it around."

"Most of humanity has been taken away from any kind of direct relationship to Earth and we've come to look at it as what *use* is it to us... What we are faced with is a whole mindset that has created a separate world for humans that runs parallel and yet isolated from the very Earth that we live on... Anything that remains now [of the land] is so precious because it is our real link to the life of this Earth... And if all that we are ever exposed to is the handiwork of man, then we will forget who we are as a species on this planet."

React and Respond

1. How have Guujaaw's experiences shaped his perspective on sustainability?
2. Select one phrase or sentence from the quotes that is especially meaningful to you. Tell why.

MEDIA FILE

Make a list of visual and print media texts that Guujaaw might use to share his perspective. Think about the way you react as the audience to each idea on your list. Take the phrase or sentence you chose in Question 2, and use it to create an advertisement (e.g., poster, internet pop-up).

Know Your WILD Neighbours

Get Ready

- Think about what is important. As you read the poems and view the art, ask what each poet and artist wants readers to believe.

CANADIAN ARTIST AND NATURALIST Robert Bateman believes that caring about our environment begins with knowing about it. To get to know our neighbours of other species, we must get outside and experience nature for ourselves. The Get to Know program, inspired by Bateman's **philosophy**, is all about raising a **generation** that cares about conservation. Each year the program holds a poetry and art contest. One year, the artists were asked to submit entries on the theme of backyard neighbours. The poets had to answer the question, "What kind of future do you want for Earth?" Here are just some of the winning entries.

philosophy a set of general life principles

generation a group of people born in a certain time frame or span of years

Untitled

Our earth aches and moans
with every step we take,
every mistake we make,
the waste we create,
we see our future dissipate.
The world abused
and bruised,
By human hand,
Destroying land,
Our dying mother
We have no other.

Jessica Wager, age 16
New Westminster, BC

Moose
Enzo Marceau, age 13
Danville, QC

Common Raccoons
Andy Lee, age 17
Surrey, BC

I want to stay

Why do we always adulterate,
Contaminate?
Phosphate, litter, other wastes,
Seem concealed,
Like it's not a big deal,
This affects our planet,
We should ban it,
It ruins our lives,
We should connive,
A way,
So we can all stay.

Tiffany Tuttle, age 14
Oshawa, ON

Fox
Jonathan Johnstone, age 16
North Sydney, NS

untitled

The boy
Threw his candy bar wrapper
Under the tree
Neglect
The girl
Revved her SUV
Out of the driveway
Obliteration
I
Picked up the wrapper and walked
Through the park
Wonder
Earth
Won't be dirty
Because of me

Jen Serdetchnaia, age 15
Newmarket, ON

Male House Finch
Joel Zelt, age 13
Kingston, ON

Salmon in the river
Olivia Truong, age 13
Toronto, ON

Sustainability

It's dying, it's dwindling
Our ability to sustain
To keep the world in existence
To keep our Earth maintained
We need to stop corrupting
Start treating it with care
To ensure in the future years
The world will still be there

Melissa Smith, age 18
Bjorkdale, SK

Crab
Heather Smith, age 17
Antigonish, NS

React and Respond

1. How does this collection of poetry and art reflect Robert Bateman's belief that "caring begins with knowing"?
2. Draft your own poem or sketch an image to show your personal response to this belief.

Build Word Power

3. Use the information in the first two sentences of the introduction to create a definition of "naturalist." Start your definition this way: "A naturalist is someone who..." Try to make your definition as complete and concise as possible. When you are finished, compare your definition with a dictionary definition and add any information that you missed.

MEDIA FILE

Create your own poem or image to show how you feel about the environment. Then, with a partner, discuss why poetry and images are good forms to present environmental concerns.

Make A Speech

We impact our global environment in many ways. More and more people are starting to believe that we have to take responsibility for our actions. Issues about the environment bring out strong opinions and points of view.

Prepare a Speech

Purpose

You create a speech to influence the opinions and actions of others.

How to do it

- Choose an issue that you care about.
- Research to find a range of views on the issue.
- Decide on your opinion and write it down in a clear statement.
- Draft your speech.
- Get feedback and revise your speech.

HINTS

When creating a speech...

- Use language that appeals to people's emotions.
- Use your voice to grab and hold the attention of your audience.
- Use facial expressions and gestures to emphasize important ideas.

TRY THIS

Prepare a speech to present your point of view on an environmental issue. Can you persuade others to feel strongly about your issue and to act on it?

Use techniques to persuade your audience to agree with your point of view and convince them that you care about the issue.

Present your speech to a group of students.

REFLECT ON SPEAKING

What steps helped you prepare to speak in a formal situation?

Blessing Song

by Lee Maracle

Get Ready

- Preview the selection. Use the art and the title to predict what the reading is about.
- Visualize. As you read, picture in your mind the images the author creates with her words.

As the boat chugs away from the dock, the salt sea air surrounds us. It invades the very pores of our skin. The sun dances across the ocean. Puget Sound—home of the giant octopus—resting place for killer whales on their migration to California, is the garden of generations of Salish people. We are witnesses who have journeyed from the sky world to this place of continuous transformation, this place of physical engagement of the sea. Mountains rise sharp, snow-capped and deep green. They circle the sound cradling this bowl of ocean, which is very nearly land locked. The depths of the sound comfort the whales. An abundance of sockeye and spring salmon attracts them here. Two of the longest and most powerful rivers on this continent drain into the sound.

We have come to watch the whales, my granddaughter, my daughter, and myself. My daughter stands more erect than I have seen her stand for a long time, a smile etched on her face as she looks out toward the sea. She rocks gently back and forth while her daughter, darts about, taking pictures with her small camera, a gift from her aunt. Tania turns to look at me, the richness of her joy is contagious. We laugh out loud.

We are where we were always meant to be, on a small boat plying the ocean waters off the West Coast of British Columbia and Washington state.

It strikes me as odd that we have opted to take a holiday that is so modern and tourist-like and yet we feel so old and so Salish for having done it. She slips her thin arm in mine, looks across at me, eyes brimming with tears of joy. We stay like that rocking back and forth as though readying ourselves for song. The sun keeps climbing the skyline, nipping at the skin. The cool winds calm the heat of the sun as she reaches her noonday **zenith**. My skin is browning under her glare, but it is not an unbearable heat. The other tourists scamper under the protection of the ship's **canopy**. They are white and so burn red under the brightness of the sun. Inside the canopy, they engage one another in conversation about the beauty of the mountains, their awesome strength, but me and my girls quietly watch and wait.

The water slaps at the boat; the waves deepen as we come closer to the congregation. The boat rocks with a growing will. We look at one another and chuckle. Our grip on one another's arm tightens. On the horizon, we see them: a super pod of resident killer whales. The water amplifies their resonant voices. There must be a hundred or more. The rocking of the boat intensifies. The waves caused by the diving whales lick at the sides and threaten to douse the boat. The captain tells us the water is going to get rougher if we try to get closer, there are so many of them.

"What's your pleasure?" he asks.

"How much closer can we get without capsizing?" someone asks him.

"Let's see." He manoeuvres the boat in the direction of the gathering.

"You may want to come inside!" He hollers at us.

"Not a chance!" We answer back at the same time and laugh.

My granddaughter stands behind us as though we would actually protect her. A small pod breaks away from the larger

zenith highest point in the sky

canopy covering to provide shelter

gathering and meanders toward the boat. The captain slows the boat down. The noisy tourists are now quiet. They lean toward the door of the cabin, clutching one another in silence. We stand pressed up against one another. The biggest of the whales swims within two metres of the boat and stands straight up and murmurs at us. The captain is stunned. "This has never happened before. He has never come this close to the boat."

The songs of my people must have come from this whale. I feel a song being pulled from me from some place deep inside. I hesitate. We don't sing in front of white people, but the killer whale seems to demand nothing less.

The song emerges from my daughter and me as we stand there before this mammoth. Both of us sing the oldest Salish song we know. The very moment the song ends, the whale slaps the water. The spray douses us and we break into laughter. He turns to join the super pod. The other whales follow him. We remain quiet and just stand there, arms still locked together. My granddaughter tells us that she has a picture of the big whale when he came up close to the boat. Her eyes sparkle with excitement. The people on board the boat are excited about what happened and curious about the song.

"It's just a song," we tell them. Neither of us is prepared to break the spell that this moment has created for us. This whale managed to close all the spaces between us. The song forced from us by the whale reminds us that our lineage stretches back forever. It isn't the song though that matters. What matters is the closing of the gap between us, the creation of oneness between three generations of Coast Salish women doing what every generation before us has done: standing in the middle of the sea singing to the whales.

React and Respond

1. Explain the significance of the encounter with the whales for the three women. What details are included in the text to support your thinking?
2. With a partner, identify the different sensory descriptions used by the author that helped you visualize the experience. Describe what her words made you see, hear, smell, taste, touch, or feel.

SPEAKER'S FILE

Select one moment of the experience to discuss in a group. Then, share your ideas with the class.

- Why is this an important moment?
- What mood is being conveyed?
- If you were directing a movie, how could you use music, light, and camera angles to communicate the meaning of this event?

Analyze Perspectives In Media

Media producers are paid to communicate specific messages to specific audiences. When reading or viewing media, take a critical stance. Identify the producers' perspectives below and consider how they achieved them.

Industry
GROWTH
Managing emission controls
New SUV to be produced in Canada: 1500 jobs announced!
Big business: Scapegoats for global warming!
Oil and gas industry events
SustainAbility
Push towards an "electric" future
Live Earth concert rocks the globe!
Green choices at the mall
Rainforest destruction rises from increased mining

TRY THIS

Work with a partner to analyze a print, TV, or web-based magazine on the environment.

Analyze a Magazine

Describe key images and words on the cover or opening image.

- Flip through the magazine looking at titles, images, and advertising. Read the contents page.
- Notice who is included and who is missing.
- Find out who produced the magazine.
- Ask yourself what the producer wants you to think. Consider how that matches with what you already know and believe.

HINTS

- What is the first thing you notice when you look at the article? Why does it stand out to you?
- What words or images have an impact on you?
- How did the producer use placement, size, and colour to make particular ideas important?

Present your findings to a small group.

- State your conclusion (i.e., what you believe the producer of the magazine wants you to think).
- Support your conclusion with evidence.

REFLECT ON MEDIA

Describe how reading, assessing, and discussing perspectives in media help you judge the effectiveness of media texts.

Excerpt from

An Island of My Own

by Andrea Spalding

Get Ready

- Visualize. What does the phrase *ocean forest* bring to mind?
- Make connections. As you read, connect the story to what you already know about endangered species.

Fifteen-year-old Rowan is the daughter of environmental journalists who are on assignment in Africa. She goes to spend the summer with her cousins, Bevan and Darcy, in an isolated area near Tofino, BC. Desperate for a summer project and a chance to prove herself to be a researcher like her parents, she camps out on a neighbouring island. There, she monitors the progress of an endangered group of sea otters threatened by real-estate development plans.

ROWAN WOKE FEELING UNCOMFORTABLE. THE SUN WAS beating in her face, sweat trickled down her neck, and her backrest had developed a prominent spike that was digging into her back. She stretched stiffly, stood up and looked out across the water. A flash caught her eye. There seemed to be something splashing out by the kelp bed near the entrance to the cove.

Rowan mentally crossed her fingers, grabbed her binoculars and pack, and headed up the headland path to watch.

It was the otters. Full of wonder, Rowan lay on her stomach high above the kelp bed, pulled out her notebook and carefully wrote down what she saw.

Suddenly, Rowan's hands tightened on the binoculars in excitement. One animal came up with a sea urchin in one paw and a flat rock in the other. It rolled onto its back and began hammering the sea urchin against the rock, then slurped out the innards as though eating ice cream from a cone. Rowan pulled out her camera, focused the zoom lens and started clicking.

This was not river otter behaviour!

"Go slowly," she told herself. "Document carefully, or people aren't going to believe you."

If she could prove this kelp bed was the home of an endangered species, maybe she could prevent the island from being sold.

Mother and pup

Sea Otter on its back eating a sea urchin

Wednesday July 3rd

Five otters in the kelp bed.

Lots of activity. Otters swimming up to the surface of the water and back down under the shiny brown kelp. They seem to be feeding. Their mouths are constantly in motion chewing fish and clams. They use their hands like we do, but they're pretty messy eaters.

As I watched, one otter came up with a sea urchin and a flat rock. He (I don't know how to tell) placed the rock on his chest then started hammering the sea urchin on it to crack open the shell. Then, he slurped out the inside (poor sea urchin) and obviously

loved it. Next it washed. The otter rolled over and over in the water, rubbed its face and cleaned its pelt, then shook its head and all the water drops fanned out from its whiskers. I guess that's what I saw the first time I noticed them.

The otters roll around in the kelp until they are wrapped in it like seat belts. Then, they lie on their backs and groom each other. They make me laugh.

Another sea otter in the middle of the kelp is not quite as active as the main group. It looks as if there is something wrong.

It's a funny shape. It's a mother with a baby lying on her chest! They are both sleeping in the sunshine. While I watched, she gently detached the baby, rolled it rapidly in kelp, then dived down into the water. I didn't know what was happening because the baby started shrieking. I thought something must be wrong, but the other otters didn't seem disturbed. A few minutes later the mother popped up with some fish. She ate, then washed, then unrolled the baby and placed it on her chest again. It instantly stopped screaming and nuzzled with its head. I guess it was nursing.

This has been a most astonishing day...

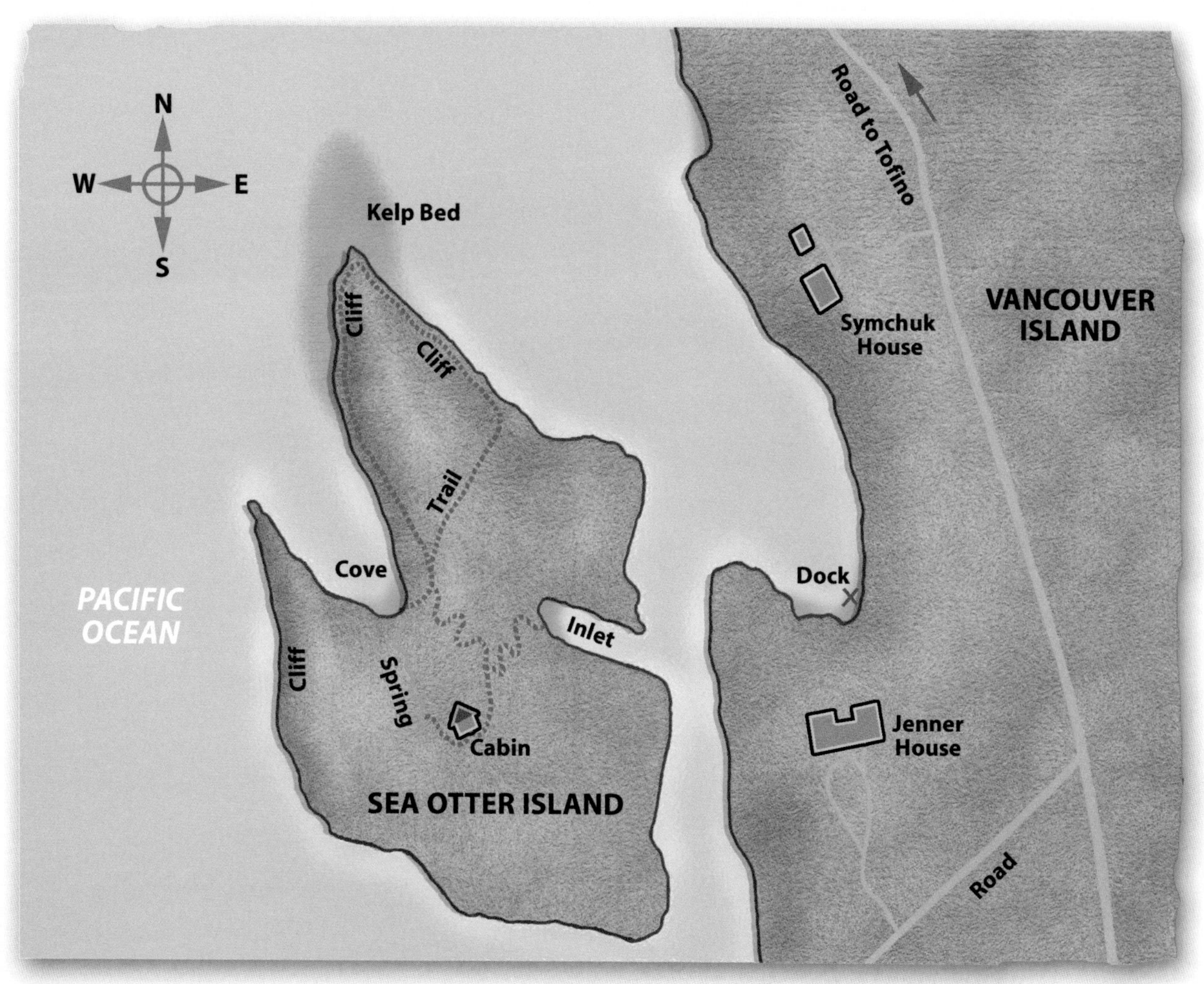

Rowan's map of Sea Otter Island

Katrina Vasey's powerboat puttered into the Jenner's landing. Bevan poked his head out of his boat's cockpit and looked across questioningly. "Hello…are you looking for someone?"

"Yes, the Jenners," Katrina shouted above the sound of the motor. "Could I dock and explain?"

"Sure." Bevan jumped out of his boat and waited for Katrina to throw a rope.

She swung gently alongside the dock and turned off the engine. Tossing the stern rope to Bevan, she leapt lightly down and secured the prow rope herself.

"Hi, I'm Katrina Vasey, a wildlife biologist from Vancouver Aquarium. Are you one of the Jenner family?" Katrina stuck out her hand.

"Yes, I'm Bevan Jenner. How did you get here so soon? I only e-mailed the aquarium last night."

"I was in the Tofino area and when I phoned in for messages this morning they read me yours." Katrina ran her finger through her hair excitedly. "I specialize in sea mammals. I was working here because several reports of sea otters came from this area."

As they walked over to the house Bevan recounted the story. "We'll phone Rowan, then go over to the island and you can see for yourself," he finished.

An excited Rowan met them on the beach. "This is wonderful," she burbled. "Mr. Symchuck is coming over tomorrow and it would be great to have a positive identification by then." She led the way up to the lookout area and gestured to everyone to be quiet.

To her delight, the otters were waiting, wrapped in a raft of kelp, snoozing on their backs, paws in the air.

Katrina started shooting film, shot after shot.

"Wonderful," breathed Katrina. She looked up from her camera with sparkling eyes. "This is exactly what I was hoping for."

"So, what do we do now?" Rowan asked.

"I need to make some observations and do a head count," Katrina smiled across at Rowan. "I'd like to see your notes and photos too."

Rowan nodded happily. "Of course."

"And I need to dive to check out the health of the kelp bed. But that will have to wait as I'm on my own."

"We could help there," Bevan interjected.

Katrina looked across, interested.

"Both Rowan and I dive and I can handle a boat. We could come with you as support."

"Have you got your **power squadron certification**?" Katrina asked Bevan.

Bevan nodded. "Mom and Dad insist we have all the mariner and diving courses. When you live out here it's almost a requirement."

Katrina considered a moment. "OK." She looked up at the sky. "The weather seems fairly settled. Rowan, would you like to be my dive partner, if Bevan will crew the boat?"

power squadron certification official certificate to operate a motor boat

"Certainly," said Rowan in her most grown-up voice, but inside her heart was racing and she felt ready to burst with excitement.

It took time to cross the channel to the Jenners' to collect and check the equipment, but by afternoon they had everything together. They swiftly loaded Rowan's gear into the boat and swung aboard.

"All set?" Katrina asked.

"You bet." Katrina set the engine in gear. They backed off smoothly from the dock and set off around Otter Island.

Sea Otter swimming in a kelp forest

The channel was smooth and still, but the moment they rounded the corner of the island the **swell** became noticeable and the wind brisker.

"Want to take over?" Katrina asked Bevan.

She watched approvingly as Bevan competently brought the boat around the far side of the island.

"Heave to about fifty metres off the kelp bed," called Katrina over the noise of the motor. "I don't want to disturb the sea otters."

Bevan anchored and dropped the flagged buoy over the side to show there was a dive in progress while Rowan and Katrina swiftly suited up.

"We'll go in on the far side of the boat, then swim toward the kelp bed and cliff," instructed Katrina. "I'll go first, but we must always stay in visual distance of each other. We will be staying at the base of the kelp. It's easy to get tangled in it so we have to be very slow and careful. If you do get caught, just disentangle, calmly."

Rowan nodded. She pulled up the hood of her wetsuit, slipped on the facemask, and gave the thumbs up sign to Katrina. They both slid over the side.

swell a long wave

Sunday July 7th

Today I acted as Katrina Vasey's diving partner, and Bevan crewed the boat. Bevan noted the surface activities of the otters from the deck, while Katrina and I dived.

We were able to ascertain there are actually seven sea otters living together as a raft, and Katrina thinks it's a group of females. All look healthy but unfortunately the pup that died seems to be the only offspring this year. However, it's impossible to tell if any of the females are pregnant and one may have a late pup. This means there must be a group of males not far away.

We officially listed all the types of sea life we observed in and around the kelp forest, and did a sea urchin count. I helped Katrina measure the forest's length and breadth. She feels it can support the otters that are there and that it should grow as the group grows.

Sea otters and sea urchins are intertwined. The otters eat the sea urchins, sea urchins eat the kelp. As long as the otters are keeping the urchin population under control, the kelp forest will expand.

Katrina says we lost thousands of kelp forests around our coast when the sea otters were hunted and wiped out. Because the sea urchins had no predator, they just ate the kelp unchecked. Once the kelp forests were gone, the safe habitat for many sea creatures was gone.

Until I dived with Katrina I had never thought of the kelp as a forest. It's changed my whole perception and view of the ocean.

Rowan closed her field notes and sat, gazing thoughtfully over the glade. The evening shadows were closing in, but there was still an air of frantic activity as a bat and a couple of swallows swooped and dove, vying with each other for the evening insect hunt.

Not even a week, that's all it had been, but this tiny island had already changed her life.

React and Respond

1. Retell the story to a partner.
2. What can you infer about Rowan's personality from her journal entries?

Build Word Power

3. Look up the origin of *urchin* in a dictionary. The word *urchin* has two different meanings: a type of sea creature and a poor or mischievious child. Why do you think this word is used in both these ways?

COMPARE TEXTS

With a partner, make a chart. Compare the language used in *An Island of My Own* with two other selections in the unit. Include the following in your chart:

- Is it factual, scientific, or emotive?
- Does the writer use powerful adjectives?
- What kind of verbs are used?
- What variety of sentence structures are used?

Discuss similarities and differences. In your opinion, which selection is the most powerful?

SHOW WHAT YOU KNOW

Create a Public Service Announcement

You are going to work in a group to create and present a one minute radio or TV public service announcement. Your announcement will raise awareness about how human actions impact Earth's environment.

Public service announcements are produced to raise awareness about important issues, such as health, safety or the environment.

Think about what you read, viewed and discussed in this unit before you begin.

Topic	*Information the public needs to know...*
Purpose	*To raise awareness of...*
Audience	*My announcement will be directed to...*
Form	*Public service announcement (e.g., TV or radio)*

PLAN YOUR ANNOUNCEMENT

List the different aspects of your announcement and decide how you will work as a group to complete it.

- Determine the form of your announcement (e.g., radio announcement or TV commercial).
- Choose roles you will take in recording or presenting.
- Write a script that will have an impact on your audience.
- Decide on ways to enhance your announcement (e.g., props, sound effects, animation, presenter).

MORE IDEAS

- Include a tagline, slogan, or song.
- Create your announcement as a podcast, audio, or video recording.

PRODUCE YOUR ANNOUNCEMENT

Put your announcement together. Work together to give feedback and revise the announcement.

Present your announcement to the class.
After your presentation, ask for feedback on what your classmates liked about the announcement, and how it could be improved.

LOOK FOR...

- a convincing message
- a form best suited to delivery of your message
- a memorable presentation
- effects that enhance your message

REFLECT

- What parts of your public service announcement were most effective?
- What does your announcement show about your understanding of purpose and audience? What else does it show about your learning?

Develop Your Portfolio

- Choose two or three pieces of work that show your learning.
- Be prepared to share them with your teacher, family and friends.

Acknowledgements

Permission to reprint copyrighted material is gratefully acknowledged. Every effort has been made to trace ownership of all copyrighted material and to secure permission from copyright holders. In the event of any questions arising as to the use of any material, we will be pleased to make the necessary corrections in future printings.

Photographs

Cover © Ron Sanford/Corbis; **1** © Ron Sanford/Corbis; **6-7** Monica Dalmasso/FirstLight; **8** Richard Wear/Design Pics/Corbis Canada; **9** top Jacques Jangoux/Getty Images; bottom Paul Glendell/Alamy; **10-11** David Woods/Corbis Canada; **12-13** left to right Roy Ooms/Masterfile; David Woods/Corbis Canada; Jacques Jangoux/Getty Images; Stephen Frink Collection/Alamy; Goodshoot/ Jupiter Images Unlimited; **12** © 2007 Daisy Gilardini / AlaskaStock.com; **13** © 2007 Daisy Gilardini / AlaskaStock.com; **14** Jean-Bernard Carillet/ lonelyplanetimages.com; **15** heading Casey Mahaney/lonelyplanetimages.com; **16** Sylvia Cordaiy Photo Library Ltd/Alamy; **17** heading Casey Mahaney/ lonelyplanetimages.com; top B Jones & M Shimlock/NHPA; centre Trevor McDonald/NHPA; bottom E.R. Degginger/Animals Animals - Earth Scenes/ maxximages.com; **18** Stephen Frink Collection/Alamy; **19** header Casey Mahaney/lonelyplanetimages.com; top Reinhard Dirscherl/Alamy; bottom Visual&Written SL/Alamy; **20** Wolfgang Kaehler Photography; **21** header Casey Mahaney/lonelyplanetimages.com; top PCL / Alamy; bottom left Mike Parry/Minden Pictures/Getty Images; bottom right David Fleetham / Alamy; **22** Photodisc / Alamy; **23** header Casey Mahaney/lonelyplanetimages.com; top right David Fleetham / Alamy; centre Adam Butler/Alamy; bottom Fred Bavandam/Minden Pictures/Getty Images; **28-29** background Maxim Tupikov/ Shutterstock; **29** top www.studentsonice.com; bottom left www.studentsonice.com; bottom right Photos.com/Jupiter Images Unlimited; **30** both www.studentsonice.com; **30-31** background Goodshot/Jupiter Images Unlimited; **31** top © 2007 Steven Kazlowski / AlaskaStock.com; bottom www.studentsonice.com; **32** John W Banagan/Iconica/Getty Images; **33** background David C Clegg/Science Photo Library; bottom Lee Foster/ lonelyplanetimages.com; **34** top David C. Clegg/Science Photo Library; bottom Michele Falzone/Alamy; **35** top G. Bowater/Corbis Canada; bottom John Tinning; Frank Lane Picture Agency/Corbis Canada; **36** top right Sinclair Stammers/ Science Photo Library; bottom left Wolfgang Kaehler/Corbis Canada; **37** top Galen Rowell/Corbis Canada; centre DLILLC/Corbis Canada; bottom Thomas Kitchin & Victoria Hurst; **38-39** left to right Roy Ooms/Masterfile; David Woods/ Corbis Canada; Jacques Jangoux/Getty Images; Stephen Frink Collection/Alamy; Goodshoot/Jupiter Images Unlimited; **38** Courtesy of Friends of Boyd Park, photograph by Anne de Haas; **40-41** Ann Johansson/Corbis Canada; **41** Christopher Morris/Corbis Canada; **46-47** left to right Roy Ooms/Masterfile; David Woods/Corbis Canada; Jacques Jangoux/Getty Images; Stephen Frink

Collection/Alamy; Goodshoot/Jupiter Images Unlimited; **52-53** left to right Roy Ooms/Masterfile; David Woods/Corbis Canada; Jacques Jangoux/Getty Images; Stephen Frink Collection/Alamy; Goodshoot/Jupiter Images Unlimited; **52** left Photos.com/Jupiter Images Unlimited; right Dave Reede/Alamy; **54-55** Roy Ooms/Masterfile; **55** Steven J. Kazlowski / Alamy; **56** top Norbert Wu Productions; bottom ThinkStock/Jupiter Images Unlimited; **58** Thomas & Pat Leeson / Photo Researchers, Inc.; **60** left Norbert Wu Productions; bottom Image Source Pink / Alamy; **61** Philip Rostron/Masterfile; inset Konrad Wothe/Minden Pictures/Getty Images; **62** J.A. Kraulis/Masterfile; **64-65** top Monica Dalmasso/ FirstLight; left Courtesy of Fisheries and Oceans Canada. Reproduced with the permission of Her Majesty the Queen in Right of Canada, 2007; centre (poster) Courtesy of WWF-Canada and (image of the polar bear on the poster) Geostock/Photodisc/Getty Images; right Ryan Schwarz.

Illustrations

12, 14, 16, 18, 20, 22, 38, 46, 53 Stephen MacEachern; **15, 28, 33, 57** Tad Majewski; **25, 27** Neil Stewart; **47** Tina Holdcroft; **50** Luc Melanson; **52** Word & Image Design; **64** François Escalmel.

Text

"Bering Sea Expedition Diary" excerpt by Margaret Williams reprinted with permission from the *World Wildlife Fund*; "Looking for Seabirds" excerpt reprinted from *Looking for Seabirds: Journal from an Alaskan Voyage* by Sophie Webb © 2004 by Sophie Webb. Reprinted by permission of Houghton Mifflin Company. All rights reserved; "Arctic Adventure" excerpts from journals and photos reprinted with permission from www.studentsonice.com; "Remarkable Rainforests" excerpt reprinted from *The Remarkable Rainforest: An Active Learning Book for Kids* by Toni Albert © 2003 Trickle Creek Books, www.TrickleCreekBooks.com; "The Rainforest Jigsaw Puzzle" excerpts from *Journey into the Rainforests* by Tim Knight (OUP, 2001), copyright © Tim Knight 2001, used by permission of Oxford University Press; "Guujaaw: An Advocate for the Planet" quotes reprinted with the permission of Guujaaw, President of the Haida Nation Council; "Know your Wild Neighbours" from the *Robert Bateman Get to Know Program*, © 2007 used by permission; "Blessing Song" by Lee Maracle, published in *Spirit Magazine*, Spring 2007 Volume 3, Issue 4; "An Island of my Own" excerpt reprinted from *An Island of my Own* © 1998. Reprinted by permission of the Dundurn Group.

Literacy in Action

AUTHORS

Arnold Toutant
Sharon Jeroski
Jean Bowman
Rick Chambers
Richard Davies
Susan Doyle
Kathleen Gregory
Raymond Lavery
Tamar Stein
Dirk Verhulst
Jerry Wowk

PEARSON
Education Canada

GRADE 7 PROJECT TEAM

Team Leader: Anita Borovilos
Publishers: Susan Green, Elynor Kagan
Research and Communications Manager: Paula Smith
Managing Editors: Caroline Kloss, Monica Schwalbe
Developmental Editor: Cathy Fraccaro
Production Editor: Marie Kocher
Production Coordinator: Sharlene Ross
Senior Manufacturing Coordinator: Jane Schell
Art Director: Zena Denchik
Designers: Zena Denchik, Word & Image Design
Permissions Research: Nadia Chapin
Photo Research: Mary Rose MacLachlan
Vice-President Publishing and Marketing: Mark Cobham

ISBN-13: 978-0-13-205903-9
ISBN-10: 0-13-205903-7

Printed and bound in Canada.
1 2 3 4 5 TC 12 11 10 09 08

The publisher has taken every care to meet or exceed industry specifications for the manufacture of textbooks. The cover of this sewn book is a premium, polymer-reinforced material designed to provide long life and withstand rugged use. Mylar gloss lamination has been applied for further durability.

CONSULTANTS

Andrea Bishop
Faye Brownlie
Caren Cameron
Maria Carty
Robert Cloney
Catherine Costello
Christine Finochio
Pat Horstead
Don Jones
Sherri Robb

SPECIALIST REVIEWERS

Aboriginal: Sheila Staats
Equity: Yaw Obeng
Levelling: Barbara Boate
Deborah Kekewich
Science: Catherine Little
Social Studies: Adolfo Diiorio
Special Education: Connie Warrender

ADVISORS AND REVIEWERS

Noreen Blake (Brampton, ON)
Jennifer Brace (Milton, ON)
Connie Bray (London, ON)
Nancy Burdeniuk (Sudbury, ON)
James Cain (Dundas, ON)
Nadine Cormack (Churchill, ON)
Kathyrn D'Angelo (Richmond, BC)
Ann Donaldson (Kanata, ON)
Pat Dooley (Nelson, BC)
Gloria Gustafson (Port Coquitlam, BC)
James Hansen (Victoria, BC)
Brian Harrison (Keswick, ON)
Douglas Hilker (Toronto, ON)
Sharon Horner (North Vancouver, BC)
Meredyth Kezar (Vancouver, BC)
Vickie Morgado (Mississauga, ON)
Nadine Naughton (Victoria, BC)
Maureen Peats (Waterloo, ON)
Bruno Pullara (Woodbridge, ON)
Tammy Renyard (Victoria, BC)
Barb Rushton (New Minas, NS)
Rey Sandre (Etobicoke, ON)
Nanci-Jane Simpson (Hamilton, ON)
Kim Smith (Newmarket, ON)
Lori Spadafora (St. Catherines, ON)
Glenn Thistle (Brantford, ON)
Max Vecchiarino (Mississauga, ON)
Raymond Wiersma (London, ON)
Marian Wilson (London, ON)

STUDENT ADVISORS

Rebecca Barrett
Kaitlyn Bell
Hazel Ann Bowhay
Bryan Cathcart
Matthew Eisen
Luke Fraccaro
Mark Fraccaro
Keith Fukakusa
Kodie Hillaire
Jordan Kovacs
Rebecca Lum
Danielle Mallozzi
Nicholas Renyard
Anton Rodrigo
Leah Rose
Kevin Seemungal
Alex Warrender
Kate Warrender
Amy Yang

In this book, you will be learning about how people survive natural disasters. *Survive!* gives you lots of opportunities to work with the whole class, with other students, and on your own.

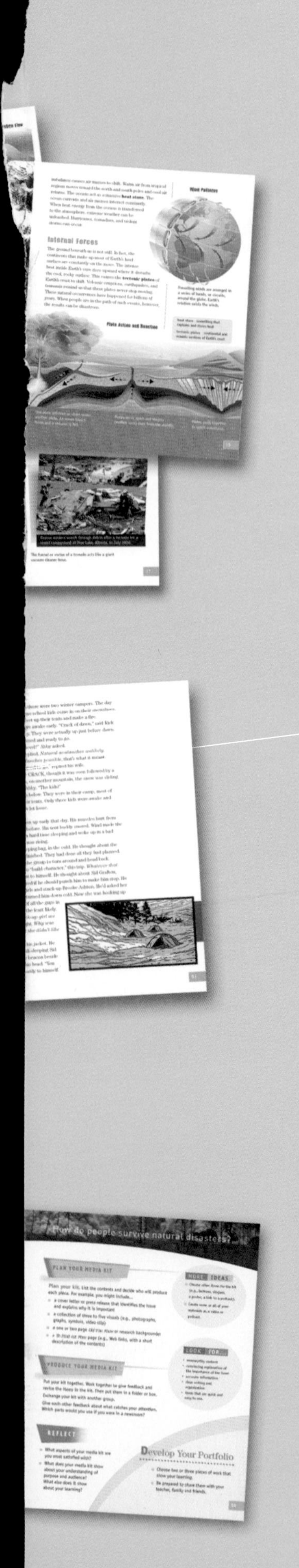

Contents

SURVIVE!

How do people survive natural disasters?

In this unit, you can...

- discuss, read, and view how knowledge of our changing planet helps people survive.
- apply comprehension strategies when you read explanations and interpret diagrams.

- write an explanation of a natural disaster.
- analyze news media to identify point of view.

At the end of the unit, you can use what you know to create a media kit.

Disasters

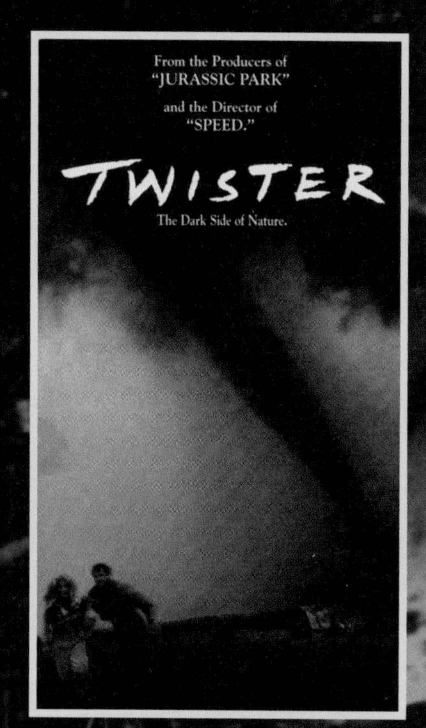

From the Producers of
"JURASSIC PARK"
and the Director of
"SPEED."
TWISTER
The Dark Side of Nature.

Get Ready

- Make connections. What images come to mind when you think about disasters?
- View with a purpose. Movie stills and posters are designed to be memorable—to create a strong feeling or reaction in viewers. What are your reactions to the movie stills and posters?

Go to the Movies

GEORGE
CLOONEY
MARK
WAHLBERG
A WOLFGANG PETERSEN FILM
THE
PERFECT
STORM
PIERCE BROSNAN
LINDA HAMILTON
DANTE'S PEAK
Whatever
You Do,
Don't Look
Back!

Sound off

1. Talk to a partner. Select the movie poster you find the most powerful and explain your choice.
2. Talk with a group. Imagine you are the producers of a new disaster movie. Brainstorm your ideas. Develop a story line and pitch your movie to the class. Ask the class to react to your movie proposal. Would they want to go and see it? Why? Why not?

When speaking...

Take turns without interrupting.

Use precise vocabulary to express ideas.

Be convincing—use concrete examples.

Repeat key points in your own words.

When listening...

Ask questions to make sure you understand.

Show interest in the ideas of others.

Summarize key ideas.

Reading Explanations

An explanation tells how and why something happens, or explains a process. Look at the explanation below and think about how you might read it.

The Structure of Earth

Layers of Earth

Earth's interior is made of rock and metal. It has four main layers.

- inner core: solid metal
- outer core: liquid and molten
- mantle: dense and mostly solid rock
- crust: thin rock material

The temperature in the core is hotter than the Sun's surface. The heat causes material in the outer core and mantle layers to move around deep inside Earth.

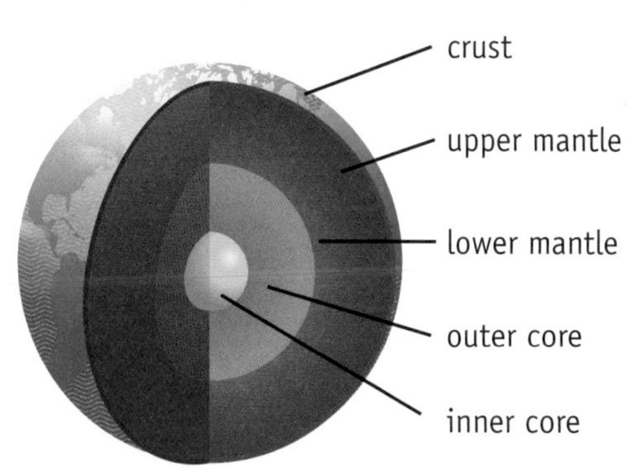

Plate Movements

Earth's crust is broken into many large and small plates that move very slowly, much too slowly to see with the naked eye. Mountain ranges are pushed up if two plates crash into each other. Other surface features are also the result of moving plates, including the shape of the continents. These movements can have dramatic effects on people and landscapes.

When you want to make connections to a selection, begin by asking...
- What do I already know about this topic?
- What have I read that is similar to this?
- Does this topic remind me of something I've seen in the media?

When you don't know the meaning of a word, look for clues by asking...
- What clues can I get from the diagrams and pictures?
- What clues can I see in the word structure?
- What other words does this remind me of?

When you want to make sure you understand what you are reading, pause and check by asking...
- What did I learn?
- Does that make sense?
- How does this information connect to what I've read before?

Interpret Diagrams

Diagrams can help you understand important ideas, if you know how to read them. **When you interpret a diagram...**

- Get an overall impression of what the diagram is about.
- Identify each part.
- Focus on the largest parts first, then move to the smaller details.
- Read the caption.
- Look for words in the caption that are also labels in the diagram.
- Ask why the author included this diagram.

Layers Inside Earth

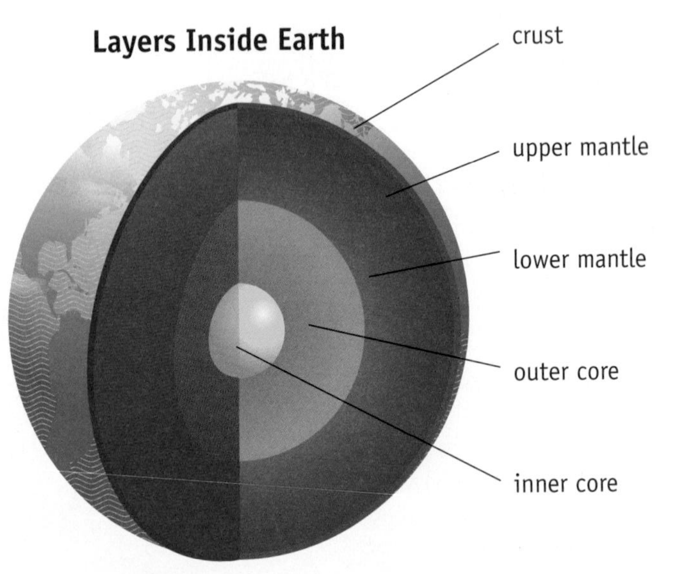

Layer temperatures increase toward the centre of Earth, from 100°C in the upper mantle to 7000°C in the inner core.

Summarize in a Graphic Organizer

You can use a graphic organizer to record ideas you are explaining or to **summarize** ideas from a text.

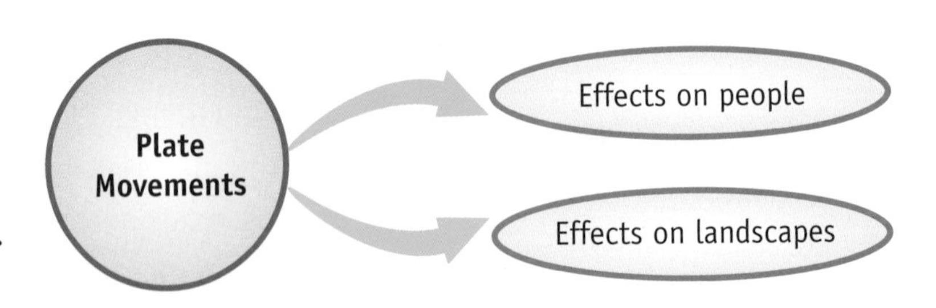

REFLECT ON READING

Which strategies will be most helpful to use when you read explanations?

Dynamic Planet

by Cathy Fraccaro

APPLY STRATEGIES

- Make connections.
- Find clues to word meaning.
- Pause and check.
- Interpret the diagram.
- Summarize.

EARTH IS A GREAT PROVIDER. IT GIVES US AIR, FOOD, warmth, and materials we need to live. Earth is constantly changing. Earth is controlled by the Sun and by the inner workings of the planet. Energy from the Sun drives the weather, and the heat from within Earth causes the movement of the rocks beneath us.

Atmospheric Forces

Earth's atmosphere is made up of layers of air masses that move around the planet. This movement creates our weather patterns. The Sun's heat powers the weather. Tropical regions receive more sunlight than the poles. This heat

imbalance causes air masses to shift. Warm air from tropical regions moves toward the north and south poles and cool air returns. The oceans act as a massive **heat store**. The ocean currents and air masses interact constantly. When heat energy from the oceans is transferred to the atmosphere, extreme weather can be unleashed. Hurricanes, tornadoes, and violent storms can occur.

Wind Patterns

Prevailing winds are arranged in a series of bands, or circuits, around the globe. Earth's rotation swirls the winds.

Internal Forces

The ground beneath us is not still. In fact, the continents that make up most of Earth's land surface are constantly on the move. The intense heat inside Earth's core rises upward where it disturbs the cool, rocky surface. This causes the **tectonic plates** of Earth's crust to shift. Volcanic eruptions, earthquakes, and tsunamis remind us that these plates never stop moving. These natural occurrences have happened for billions of years. When people are in the path of such events, however, the results can be disastrous.

heat store something that captures and stores heat

tectonic plates continental and oceanic sections of Earth's crust

Plate Action and Reaction

One plate subsides or slides under another plate. An ocean trench forms and a volcano is fed.

Plates move apart and magma (molten rock) rises from the mantle.

Plates push together to lift up mountains.

Tornadoes

APPLY STRATEGIES

- Make connections.
- Find clues to word meaning.
- Pause and check.
- Interpret the diagram.
- Summarize.

A TORNADO IS A VIOLENT STORM. IT HAS STRONG winds that whirl around in a funnel shape. It can sound like a freight train or a jet. Rain, hail, high winds, and lightning often come with a tornado. It is hard to predict when a tornado will strike. Luckily, a tornado only lasts about ten minutes. *Twisters* and *whirlwinds* are other names for tornadoes.

What Causes Tornadoes?

Tornadoes can start when a mass of warm air hits a mass of cold air. A huge thundercloud forms and rain pours down. Warm, moist air from the ground rises up towards the cloud. Cold, dry air mixes with this warmer air. This creates a churning wind.

Next, an **updraft** is formed when more warm air rushes in. This updraft sucks air away from the ground. It also makes the wind flip into a vertical funnel. This funnel stretches down and scoots along the ground. As the swirling winds pick up dirt from the ground, the funnel grows darker.

updraft upward movement of air

debris fragments of rock, soil, and earth

Effects of Tornadoes

The twisting wind of a tornado causes serious damage. A tornado's funnel is like a giant vacuum cleaner. It sucks up anything on the ground it touches. Tornadoes can lift vehicles, cut power lines, and tear off roofs. They can ruin crops and other vegetation. Even the weakest tornadoes have severe effects. They can destroy chimneys, roof shingles, satellite dishes, and tree branches. The worst tornadoes can flatten trees and crush metal buildings. Flying **debris** also causes much damage. People can be hurt or killed by a tornado strike.

Tornado Risk Areas in North America

The United States has the most tornadoes in the world. Canada is second with about 80 per year.

From Thunderstorm to Tornado

The funnel or vortex of a tornado acts like a giant vacuum cleaner hose.

Rescue workers search through debris after a tornado hit a resort campground at Pine Lake, Alberta, in July 2000.

Mudslides

IMAGINE A RIVER OF MUD ROARING DOWN A HILLSIDE. You now will have a very accurate picture of a mudslide. A mudslide is a very wet landslide. It is sometimes called a debris flow because this type of landslide carries more than just mud. It is a water-soaked (saturated) mass of soil and rocks that picks up anything in its path.

APPLY STRATEGIES

- Make connections.
- Find clues to word meaning.
- Pause and check.
- Interpret the diagram.
- Summarize.

What Causes Mudslides?

Gravity and water play a role in causing mudslides. Hurricanes and other severe rain storms produce a lot of water in a short period of time. Soil on a steep slope becomes so wet that it is too heavy to stick to the underlying rock or soil. Gravity pulls the mud down the hill. The saturated soil flows much faster and farther than an ordinary

landslide. The debris flow ranges from watery mud to thick, rocky mud that can carry large boulders and trees. Mudslides happen in places that are hilly or steep. Coastal areas with cliffs weakened by **erosion** can have mudslides when there is intense rainfall. Droughts, wildfires, and **deforestation** can destroy vegetation. There is a strong chance that these areas will also have mudslides during and after heavy rainfall.

Effects of Mudslides

Mudslides can have devastating effects on people and landscapes. They bury houses, vehicles, crops, animals, and people. On average, mudslides cause 25 to 50 deaths each year. The tides of mud, trees, and boulders can sweep through villages and towns, destroying the vegetation along the way. When the flows reach flatter ground, the debris spreads over a wide area, sometimes collecting in thick deposits. The mud will stifle any plant and animal life beneath it. Places hit by mudslides are often declared disaster areas. Nothing will live there for a long time. A mudslide can leave a deep scar on a mountainside or hillside. This acts as a reminder of potential danger to those who live nearby.

A Mudslide or Debris Flow

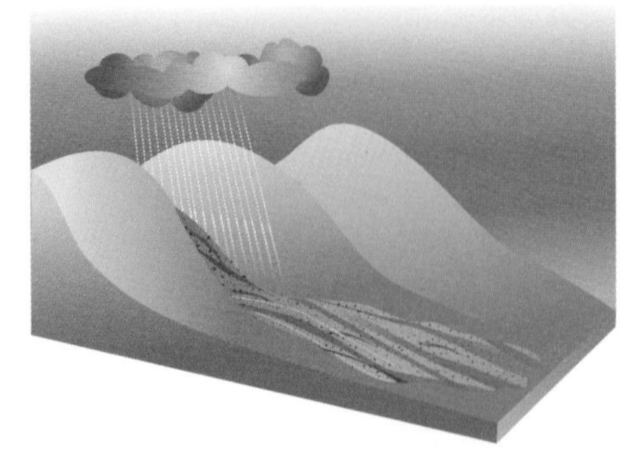

A water-soaked mass of soil and rocks becomes a debris flow.

erosion process whereby water or wind wears away Earth's surface

deforestation clearing of trees

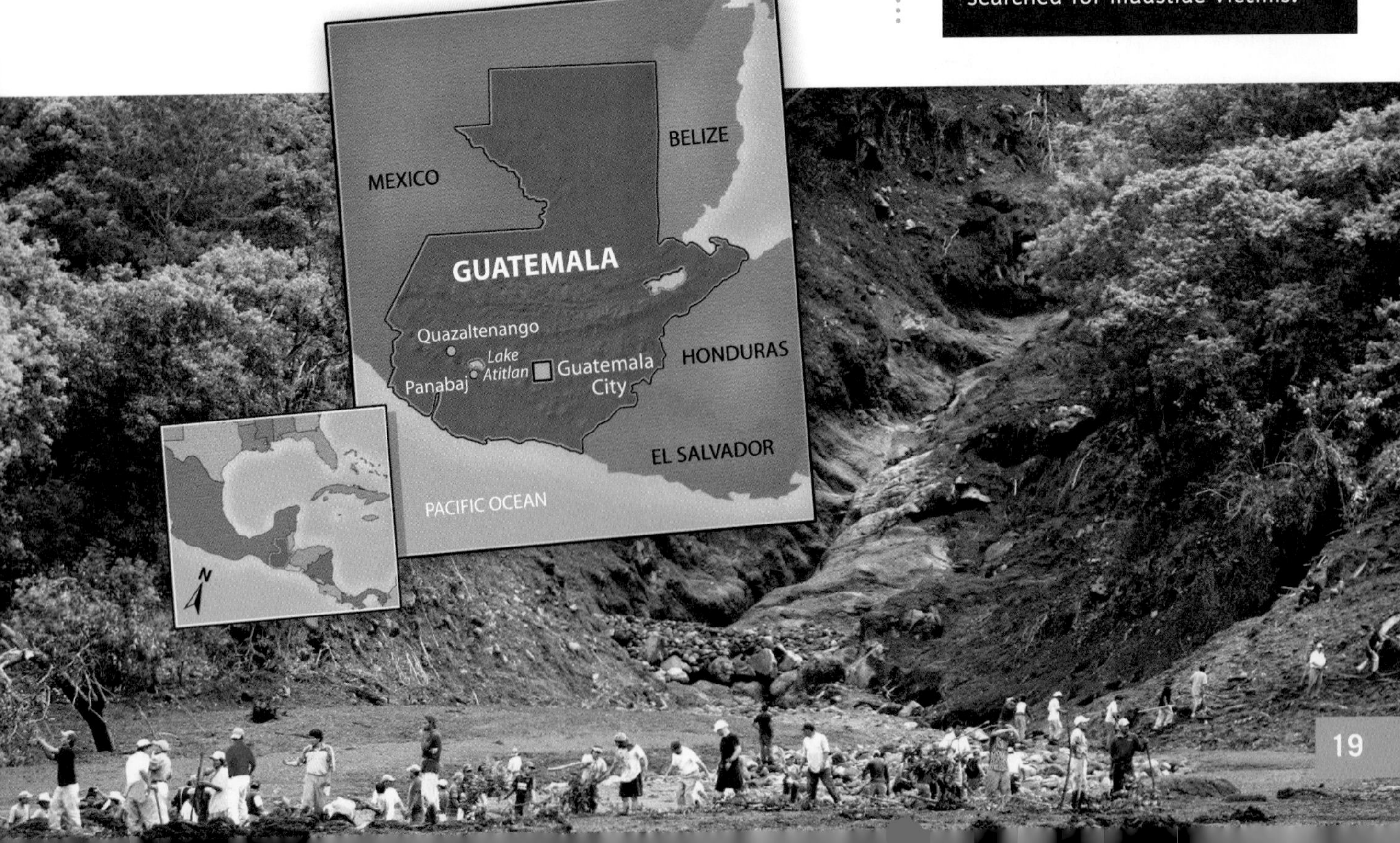

The entire village of Panabaj in Guatemala was wiped out by a mudslide in October 2005. Volunteers from neighbouring villages searched for mudslide victims.

Volcanoes

BEFORE AND AFTER A VOLCANO ERUPTS, THE ground trembles. Hot, gassy material is moving beneath Earth's crust. The air reeks of burning metal. The heat is intense. Some volcanoes, like Hawaii's Mauna Loa, erupt slowly and quietly. Others, like Mount St. Helens, in the northwest United States, erupt with great force and thunderous noise.

APPLY STRATEGIES

- Make connections.
- Find clues to word meaning.
- Pause and check.
- Interpret the diagram.
- Summarize.

What Causes Volcanoes?

Huge, solid chunks called tectonic plates make up Earth's crust. These plates float on top of Earth's molten **mantle**. A volcano is formed when **magma** from Earth's mantle breaks through the crust. It can come through weak spots in the plates or ooze out from the edges. Once the magma breaks through the crust, it is called lava. Lava flows downhill and hardens when it cools.

mantle layer of Earth beneath the crust, about 2900 km thick

magma molten or melted rock inside Earth

Effects of Volcanic Eruptions

Lava flow destroys everything in its path. Volcanic mudflows are mudslides that can bury plants, animals, and people. Sometimes bits of rock fly out of a volcano at speeds of more than 150 km/hr. These fragments, when combined with hot ash and gases, create a pyroclastic flow. Clouds of dust and ash fall to the ground after an eruption. These clouds are harmful to animals and humans. They can ruin habitats and crops. They can damage transportation and communication systems. The clouds block out some of the sun's rays and this can affect the weather.

Volcanoes are found on every continent except Australia, but more than half are in the Ring of Fire—the zone around the Pacific Ocean where different plates meet.

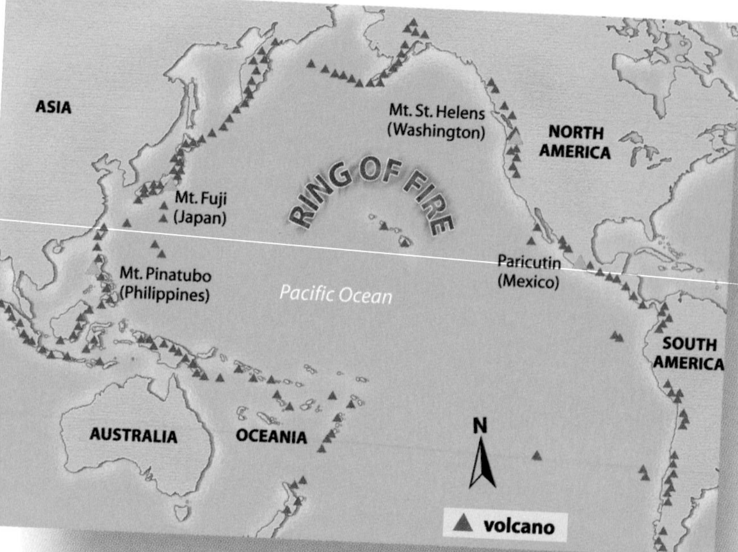

Thousands of trees were blown down or singed by the volcanic eruption of Mount St. Helens in May 1980.

The effects of a volcanic eruption can be felt for hundreds of kilometres on the ground and in the atmosphere.

Volcanic Hazard Distances

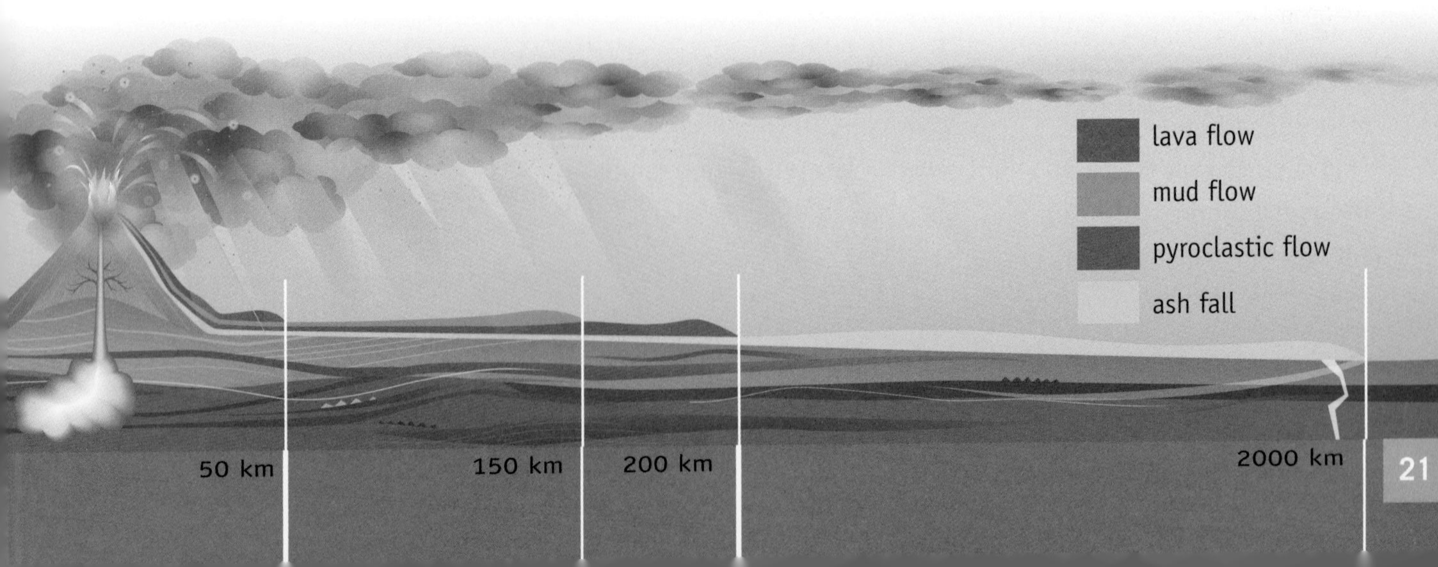

Tsunamis

APPLY STRATEGIES

- Make connections.
- Find clues to word meaning.
- Pause and check.
- Interpret the diagram.
- Summarize.

A TSUNAMI IS A FAST-MOVING OCEAN WAVE OR A SERIES of waves. In the deep ocean, a tsunami is usually no more than one metre tall. When a tsunami reaches shallow water, it can grow as high as 30 metres.

The December 2004 tsunami caused major destruction to the Indonesian region of Aceh.

What Causes Tsunamis?

An underwater earthquake, a volcanic eruption, or a landslide can trigger a tsunami. For example, when an earthquake happens, the sea floor shifts. This sudden movement creates a sea bulge that sends out a series of ripple-like waves. In the deep ocean, these ripples are very wide and low, and travel fast. They cannot be felt aboard ships, nor can they be seen from the air in the open ocean.

Effects of Tsunamis

A chain of tsunami waves can be very destructive. The pounding water can strip away sand from beaches and tear up trees and other **vegetation**. A tsunami can destroy coastal towns and villages. People can be swept away and drowned.

vegetation plant life

From Earthquake to Tsunami

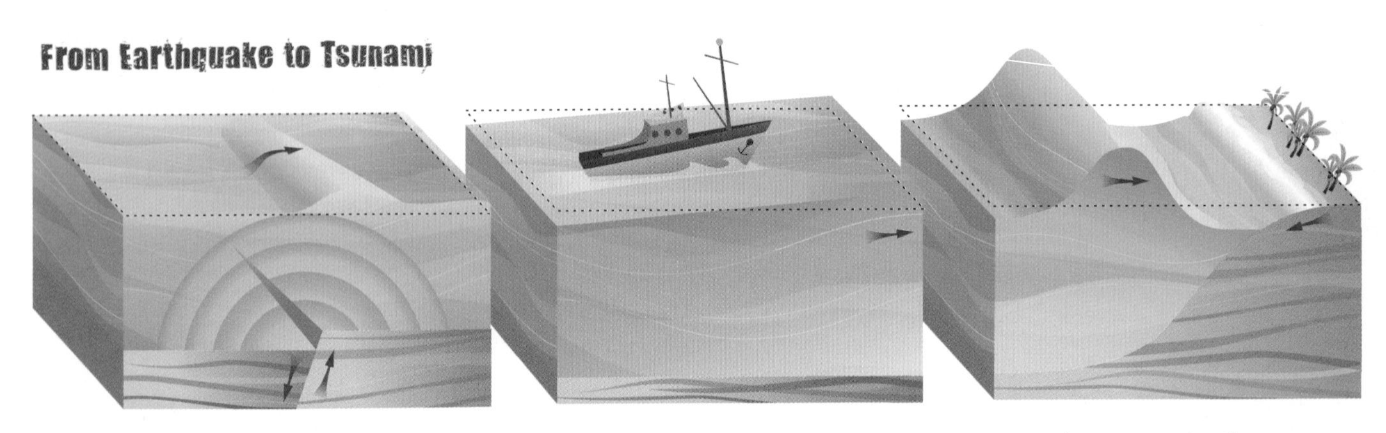

Seabed shifts due to earthquake and giant ripples are produced.

In deep water, tsunami waves travel as wide, low ripples.

Decreasing water depth causes waves to slow down and rear up, sucking water away from shore.

Nature's Warning

by Susan Blackhall

How Animals Survived the 2004 Tsunami

Get Ready

- Make connections. What do you already know about the ability of animals to sense things that we cannot?
- Ask questions. Record two questions about animals and the tsunami that you think this selection will answer.

They seemed to sense it was coming. A herd of elephants in Thailand began behaving strangely. They stamped the ground and tugged at their chains until their mighty strength freed them and they could run higher into the hills. At the same time, in the Thai resort of Phuket, a four-year-old elephant called Ning Nong was giving a tourist ride to an eight-year-old British girl, Amber Mason, of Milton Keynes, Buckinghamshire. Suddenly, a sixth sense made Ning Nong bolt from the beach up to higher ground. "I think Ning Nong knew something was wrong and was trying to get off the beach," said Amber. Her mother, who in the confusion thought her little girl had drowned, later said, "If she had stayed on the beach, she would never have lived..."

System

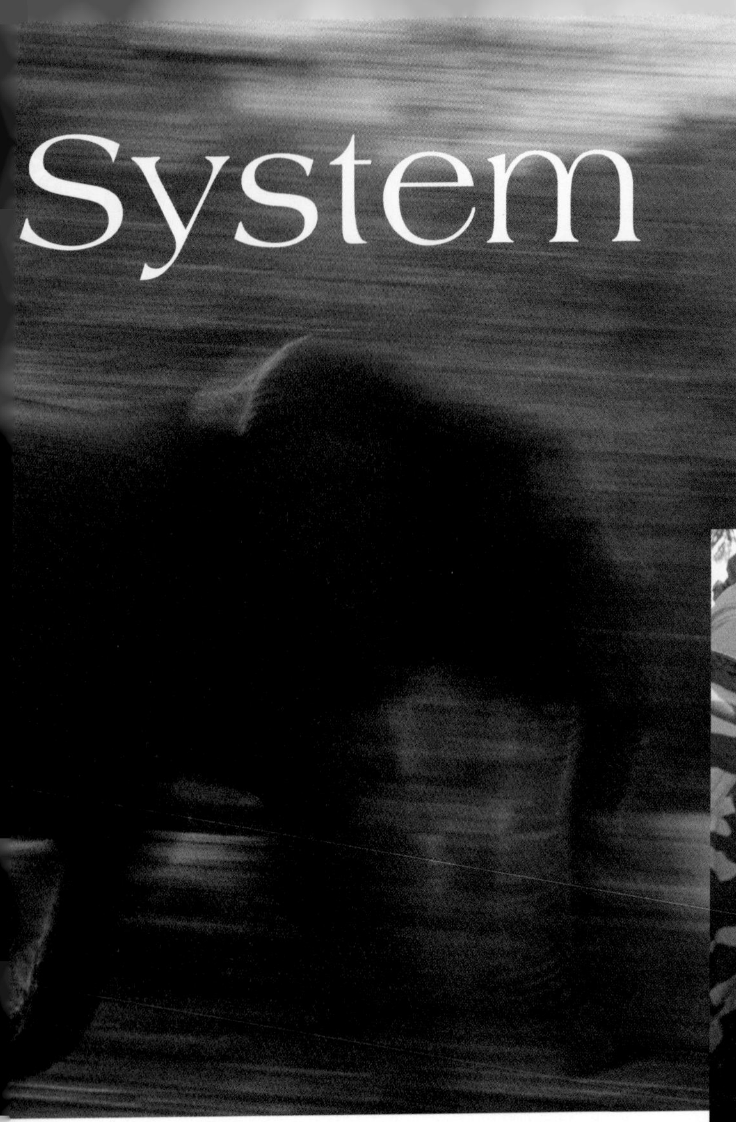

“They stamped the ground and tugged at their chains until their mighty strength freed them...”

Elephants in Khao Lak, the hardest-hit area of Thailand, trumpeted in fear three hours before the earthquake struck hundreds of kilometres away. They sounded the alarm again before the deadly wave hit. It is believed that elephants, already one of nature’s most sensitive beasts, have special bones in their feet that enable them to sense vibrations long before humans.

Meanwhile, off the coast of Thailand, professional diver Chris Cruz was leading an expedition when scores of dolphins erupted from the water, surrounded his boat, and led him farther out to sea, where he could ride the wave harmlessly rather than be swamped by it. “If we had stayed where we were, we would not have survived,” he said later.

This Indo-Pacific humpback dolphin survived the tsunami but was swept into a lake in Khao Lak, Thailand. Here a rescue team prepares to release the dolphin back into the sea.

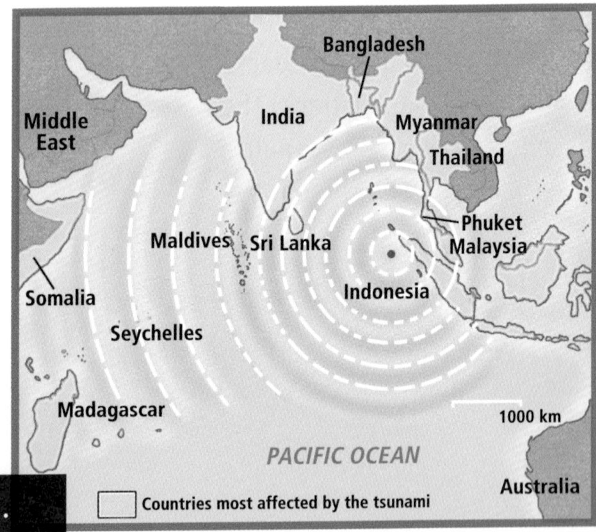

This map shows the large area hit by the tsunami.

ANIMALS KNEW

Scientists noted that the animal populations of the regions survived extraordinarily well. "No elephants are dead, not even a dead hare or rabbit," said a Sri Lankan wildlife expert. "I think animals can sense disaster. They know when things are happening."

In Indonesia, eight elephants that were part of a tourist ride were credited with saving the lives of a dozen visitors the morning of the tsunami. Immediately after the earthquake, say observers, the elephants began shifting nervously and trumpeting—something they do only when frightened. Even though their trainer calmed them, they bolted for higher ground—just moments before the first tsunami wave hit—with their frightened passengers clinging to the baskets on the elephants' backs. Had they stayed on the regular track, the animals and their riders would have certainly been killed.

Wild animals, like the Indian Hare, were aware of the approaching tsunami danger.

But there were more animal-instinct phenomena. Flamingoes abandoned their low-lying breeding areas in Thailand. At the fishing village of San Suk, birds started squawking frantically. Villagers took heed and ran, and all 1000 escaped unharmed.

A lighthouse lookout reported seeing a herd of antelope at a wildlife sanctuary in southern India stampeding from the shoreline to nearby hills just moments before the massive waves crashed across the shore. And at Malaysia's national zoo, animals could feel imminent danger in the air and refused to come out of their pens, choosing to stay sheltered instead.

Richard Mackenzie, producer of a TV program "Tsunami: Animal Instincts," which highlighted the unusual behaviour of animals leading up to the disaster, said, "This kind of behaviour was being reported in news stories at the time. But the more we looked into it, the more we realized it wasn't just a case of wild anecdotes. Eyewitness accounts by naturalists and scientists consistently showed that animals knew about the tsunami significantly before any humans realized what was coming."

Flamingoes fled from the shores to the forests before the tsunami hit.

In Sri Lanka, many thousands of people were killed—but, according to staff at the National Wildlife Department, all of the wild elephants and those that give rides to tourists, plus all of the deer, survived. Of 2000 animals in one sanctuary in India, only one, a boar was killed.

Biologist Dr. Mike Heithaus explained his theory on the eerie sense that animals seemed to have when the tsunami was imminent. "Wild animals are extremely sensitive," he said. "They have excellent hearing and they probably heard the killer waves coming in the distance. There's also vibration. And there may have been changes in the air pressure which alerted animals and made them move to safer ground."

Richard Mackenzie is more succinct in his opinion of an animal's built-in "danger radar" when a tsunami is about to hit. "Even seconds in a situation like that could, without question, have meant the difference between life and death," he said. "I guess the lesson is that we have to take them more seriously and not be afraid to wonder what they're doing, why they're doing it, and what they might be trying to tell us."

React and Respond

1. Make a list of the evidence from this selection that animals have early warning systems.
2. How convincing is the author's evidence that animals have a sixth sense? Did she convince you? Why or why not?

Build Word Power

3. A sixth sense is a sense beyond our usual five senses. The adjective "extrasensory" has the same meaning. *Extra* comes from Latin, meaning "beyond" and *sensory* means "of our senses." Use a thesaurus to find five synonyms for the word "extrasensory."

WRITER'S FILE

- Read like a writer. How is the information in this selection organized? What words and phrases make the organization clear?
- Work with a partner. Use the information from the selection to write a brief news report to explain one of the following events. Write your report as breaking news.
  - elephants in Khao Lak
  - Chris Cruz and the dolphins
  - the birds in the fishing village of San Suk

Learning from Tragedy

by Jeff Groman

Izmit 1999

Get Ready

- Think about what you already know. How do earthquakes affect people and communities?
- Set a purpose. How could the information in this selection be useful to you?

In the early hours of the morning on August 17, 1999, most people in the Turkish city of Izmit were asleep in their beds. Then, at 3:01 A.M., an earthquake originating at a depth of 17 km and with its **epicentre** about 11 km from Izmit, hit the surface and the whole town shook. Within seconds buildings began to collapse, killing thousands of people as they slept and leaving tens of thousands homeless.

The earthquake measured 7.4 on the Richter scale and produced up to 60 km of cracks in Earth's surface. The damage to buildings in most of the affected areas was very extensive. Over 60 000 residential buildings and 10 000 businesses were destroyed. Hundreds of schools and many hospitals were damaged.

Collapsed buildings in Izmit—as much the result of poor construction as the force of the quake.

epicentre point on Earth's surface directly above the focus of an earthquake

Why Did the Buildings Fall?

As Turkish rescue teams worked around the clock to try to reach victims trapped in the rubble, public anger grew as to why so many buildings were not able to withstand the effects of the quake. With over 1000 rural migrants flowing into Izmit and Istanbul every day, it is believed that cheaply built housing was mainly responsible for the high death toll. A total of 65 percent of all buildings in Turkey are constructed without an official permit. Older buildings made of solid material withstood the quake, while modern mud-brick structures folded like card houses.

Rebuilding in Izmit

After the earthquake, tent cities were set up to house the homeless. Those who had homes were afraid to go inside for fear of aftershocks. Many people moved and never returned. Those who stayed tried to rebuild this once very prosperous area.

Perhaps the earthquake's impact would not have been so devastating, if the city's buildings had been more shock absorbent. It is possible to fool earthquakes and reduce their effects by following some important structural guidelines.

Rescue operations in Izmit—a race against time with air running out for survivors trapped under rubble. The possibility of aftershocks is ever present in the rescuers' minds.

TURKISH QUAKES

- It is thought that more than 25 000 people perished in an earthquake in Antioch (modern Antakya) in C.E. 526.
- Over the past 75 years, more than 20 Turkish quakes have exceeded 6.0 on the Richter scale.
- In 1939, a quake in Erzincan in the east of the country killed more than 30 000 people.
- A 1997 study estimated a 12 percent chance of a quake hitting Izmit before 2020.

Protecting Buildings from Earthquakes

Many different materials are used to construct buildings—steel, reinforced concrete, wood, stone, and bricks. Structural engineers make sure that these materials do not collapse under the force of an earthquake. They rely on basic structural properties, such as **flexibility** and **ductility**.

An earthquake-resistant structure should be flexible. Think of a tall tree in the wind. The tree bends a little as the wind pushes against it, and when the wind stops, the tree straightens up again, unharmed. Copying nature, structural engineers have found ways of using materials to make buildings in earthquake zones more flexible.

The second important structural property is ductility (see the *Bend It* activity on page 32). In earthquake-prone areas, steel bars are added to brittle concrete during construction to increase its ductility.

In addition to making buildings more flexible and ductile, other methods have also been used to help fool earthquakes. Buildings can be cut away or isolated from the ground, letting them float while the ground moves under them.

flexibility the ability of a material to be bent under force repeatedly without breaking

ductility the ability of a material to be bent

- In 1998, a quake in the city of Adana killed 144 people and injured more than 1500.
- On November 12, 1999, a quake measuring 7.2 on the Richter scale hit the city of Düzce, Turkey, killing over 400 people and destroying buildings.
- The Agri province in Turkey was shaken by a moderate 5.0 magnitude earthquake on January 21, 2007. There were no deaths but several villages suffered damage.

Other buildings are put on springs or rubber pads (see the *Pad It* activity on page 33). Pads used in buildings are made of alternating layers of hard rubber sheets and steel plates. They act like giant hockey pucks that squish as the building rocks on top of them, absorbing some of the energy caused by the shaking. Many buildings in California and Japan are now protected from earthquake damage by sitting on these pads.

To prevent the destruction caused by earthquakes in the future, it is necessary to build new shock-absorbent structures and to reinforce older buildings. The rebuilding in Izmit continues today, so that the city is better prepared should an earthquake strike again.

BEND IT

Take a piece of chalk and try to bend it: it will snap (Fig. 1). Now take a paper clip and bend it back and forth: it will bend a number of times before it breaks (Fig. 2).

We say that the paper clip is *ductile* and the chalk is *brittle* (it behaves like glass that shatters when hit).

It takes more work to break the paper clip than the chalk, which means you used more energy breaking the paper clip. In the same way, steel absorbs quite a bit of an earthquake's energy before breaking, while concrete breaks without absorbing much earthquake energy.

Figure 1

Figure 2

Source (Bend It and Pad It): *Earthquake Games* by Matthys Levy and Mario Salvadori

People sit outside a destroyed house. In contrast, the mosque in the background stands unharmed by the earthquake.

Just after the earthquake in 1999, these families in Istanbul prefer to live outside for fear of aftershocks. Later, it became necessary to erect tent cities for those who had no homes to return to. (Inset) A young girl sits outside her tent in Izmit despite the heavy rain.

React and Respond

1. Make a chart to identify the kinds of information you found in the various text features.
2. Work with a partner. Use the images to explain how the 1999 earthquake in Izmit affected the lives of the people and the landscapes in the area.

Build Word Power

3. Ductility contains the important Latin root *duct* (or *duc*), which means "lead." How does the meaning of the root help you understand the meaning of "ductility"? What other words do you know containing the root *duct*?

WRITER'S FILE

- Read like a writer. How does the author use details about the human impact of the earthquake to make the selection memorable?
- Write a letter to the editors of a Turkish newspaper explaining why building standards that require earthquake-resistant construction are important for their region. Work with a partner to revise your letter to make your explanation clear.

PAD IT

Cut two pads the width of a cereal box from a 5 cm thick soft foam sponge and glue them to the bottom of the cereal box (Fig. 3).

Glue the bottom of the pads to a sheet of cardboard. Fill the cereal box with sand or stones to give it inertia (the tendency of an object to resist a change in motion).

Shake the cardboard slightly but quickly. The cereal box remains practically unmoved. It is partially isolated from the cardboard "earth" and returns exactly to its original position (Fig. 4).

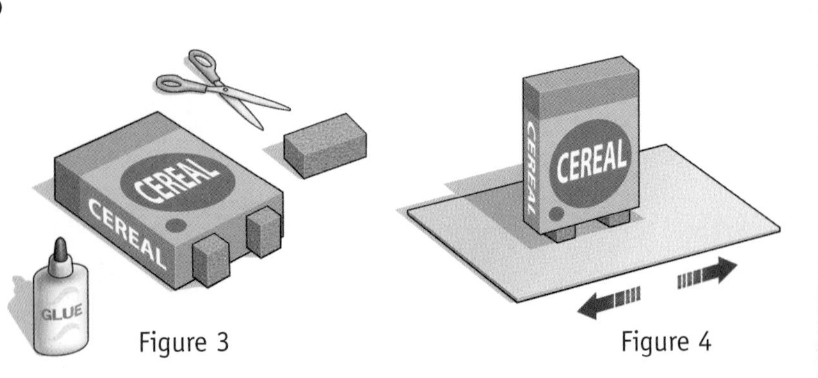

Figure 3

Figure 4

Avalanche Alert!

by Claire Watts and Jack Challoner

Avalanches are a major mountain hazard. This powerful force of nature is capable of snapping trees like match sticks and burying people and buildings in its path.

Two avalanches in Austria in 1999 caused more than 30 deaths.

Effects of Avalanches

Avalanches can have damaging effects on the landscape and on people. Trees, buildings, and living things that lie in the path of an avalanche can be swept away. Villages, hamlets, and resorts are buried or cut off from communication. Every year, avalanches claim hundreds of lives and injure many others.

Get Ready

- Preview the selection. How is the information about avalanches organized?
- Make connections. What reading strategies might help you understand and remember this information?

How Does an Avalanche Start?

An avalanche starts when mountain snow builds into an unstable overhang or becomes loose because of a thaw. Triggered by an earth tremor or by a loud noise, the avalanche grows as it rolls down the slope, loosening more snow and picking up rocks and soil. The path of an avalanche can be 800 metres wide.

Forecasting Avalanches

In regions prone to avalanches, it is important to monitor the stability of the snow. Forecasters build snow pits so that they can examine the layers. An avalanche is more likely to occur if any of the layers contains air or is made up of ice pellets. These pellets can roll over each other, allowing large slabs of snow above to break away. Although it is difficult to predict exactly when and where an avalanche will take place, experts can tell when the snow layers begin to become unstable enough to trigger an avalanche.

Preventing Avalanches

Artificial barriers of wood, concrete, or metal built across the slopes can bring tumbling snow to a halt before it has a chance to grow into a huge avalanche. Sometimes explosives are used to trigger small, controlled avalanches. This prevents the buildup of large snow masses that could cause a major avalanche.

Avalanche-Prone Areas of the World

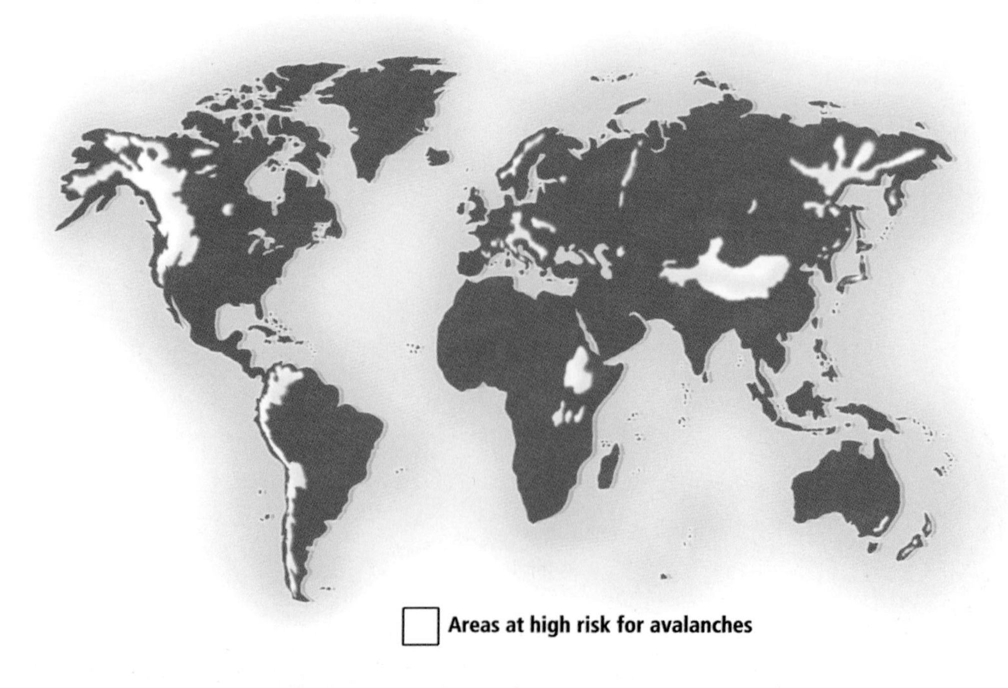

Skiers and hikers sometimes trigger avalanches.

Rescue

Anyone caught in an avalanche has just a five percent chance for survival. Speedy rescue is essential to save any survivors buried under the dense snow. For hundreds of years, rescue teams have used specially trained dogs to find trapped people. With their highly developed sense of smell, dogs are still more efficient than any electronic sensor, although many back country skiers now carry personal radio beacons in case they are buried by an avalanche.

Rescue teams use helicopters to reach injured people quickly. A winch is used to lower rescuers and haul up the injured on stretchers. The pilot must be very careful, because even the noise and rotor wash of a helicopter can trigger another avalanche.

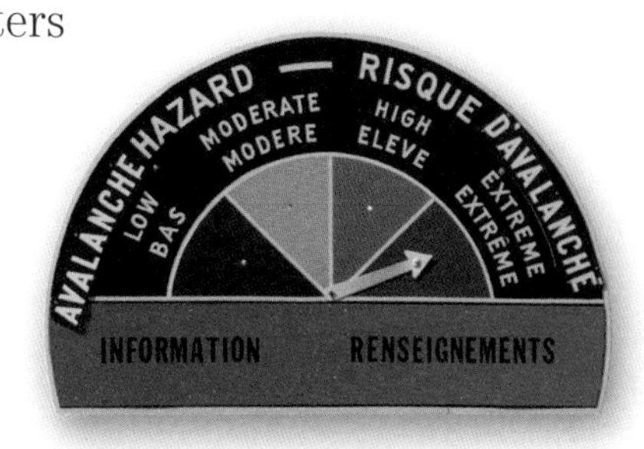

In mountain ski resorts, warning signs indicate the risk of avalanches.

An avalanche path in the Canadian Rockies

The Himalayas have more avalanches than any other place on Earth. Tibetan sherpas, or mountain guides, hang pieces of cloth to please the mountain spirits and ward off avalanches.

A rescue dog digs out an avalanche victim.

React and Respond

1. What dangers do rescue teams need to consider during a rescue?
2. Discuss ways to raise peoples' awareness of avalanches.

Build Word Power

3. When a region has frequent avalanches, we say it is "avalanche-prone." Use *–prone* to create other adjectives (e.g., someone who often has accidents).

WRITER'S FILE

- Read like a writer. What special features did the writer use (e.g., headings, visuals)?
- With a partner, make a list of important information avalanche teams need to know. Create a title and write the first paragraph of a booklet to provide guidelines for avalanche teams.

Writing Explanations

Nicole wrote a newspaper article to explain the cause and effects of an ice storm. Look at Nicole's task outline, her final draft, and some comments she made about her work.

Natural Disaster	*Ice Storm*
Purpose	*To inform*
Audience	*Other students in my class*
Form	*Newspaper article*

I used the features of a real news article: strong title, captions, and a visual.

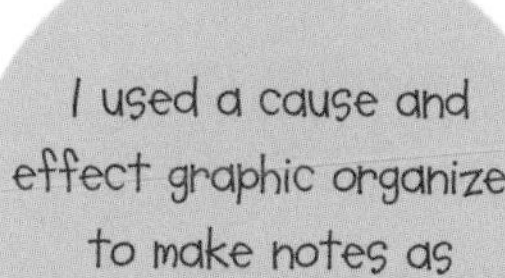

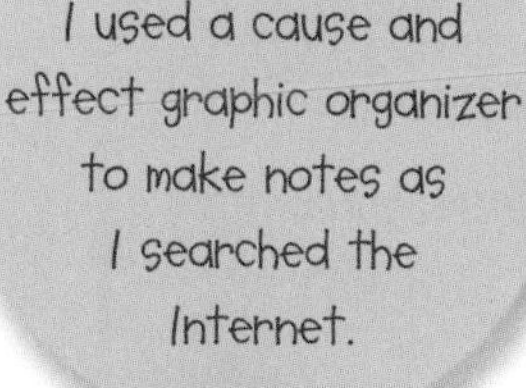

I used a cause and effect graphic organizer to make notes as I searched the Internet.

ICE STORM PARALYZES QUEBEC!

by Nicole Chu

Montreal–A severe ice storm has hit the province and may last another few days according to weather forecasters. Freezing rain is still falling in Quebec, Ontario, New Brunswick, and parts of the northeastern United States.

How freezing rain is formed

Freezing rain happens when a warm air mass full of moisture meets a cold air mass. Snow melts as it falls through layers of warm air. These droplets turn to ice when they hit cold air closer to the ground. Everything gets covered in a layer of ice.

Trees and power lines have come down under the weight of the ice. Many hydro towers have been damaged. Over three million people are without electricity and heat today. It is very dangerous to go outside in this weather. The airport is closed and so are schools and businesses. Farmers are worried about their animals because the barns cannot be heated.

Emergency workers are busy clearing the roads and restoring power. People are being advised to stay safely inside and to help their neighbours if possible.

HINTS

- Use a graphic organizer to guide your writing.
- Start with a clear statement about the phenomenon you will explain.
- Start a new paragraph for each main idea.

Write An Explanation

It's your turn to write an explanation of a natural disaster.
Ask yourself the following questions:

- What kind of disaster will I write about?
- What will my purpose be?
- Who will read my writing?
- What form will my writing take?

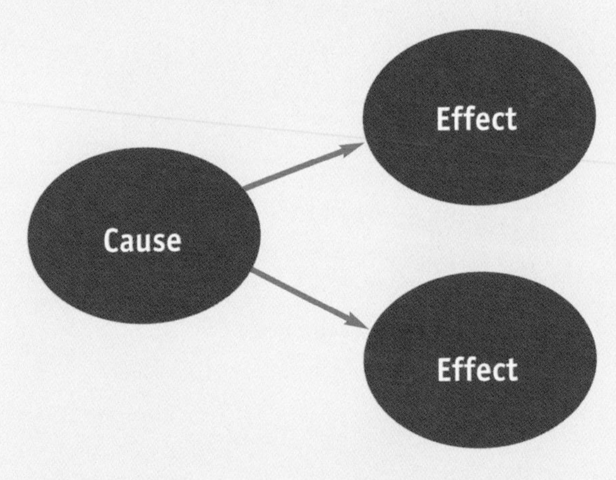

Use a cause and effect graphic organizer to take notes for your explanation.

REFLECT ON WRITING

How will you assess your explanation? Record three key criteria that will help you. Assess your explanation using these criteria.

- What aspect was most successful?
- What aspect will you need to work on?

NATURAL DISASTERS

by Marilyn Singer

We were talking disasters
scaring ourselves
with what on earth would scare us:
Volcanoes venting red-hot rivers
spumes of ash
like barbecues gone crazy
Earthquakes that crack the world
like a walnut
Sandstorms that suffocate
Tidal waves that drown
Hurricanes, tornadoes
avalanches, floods

Get Ready

- Visualize. As you read this poem, imagine that you are part of the poet's conversation. What would you be thinking and feeling?

And blizzards
simple blizzards —
those frightened me the most
trapping me right there in my house
with nothing to eat
but my shoes
We were talking disasters
feeling the earth go wobbly
leaving ourselves
with no place to hide
Until right outside my window
a robin chirruped loudly
in the hickory tree
like nothing on earth mattered
but its song
And suddenly the room righted itself
the floor held steady
and we knew that we were safe
for at least another day

React and Respond

1. What idea about natural disasters is conveyed by the phrase "for at least another day"? What made the speaker know that they were safe?
2. List at least five examples of unusual comparisons or figurative language to convey strong images and feelings. Create two other comparisons the poet could have made.

SPEAKER'S FILE

Work with a small group to present the poem. Consider how you can use your voices in your presentation (e.g., one, two, or all voices; quiet or loud voices; repeat words, phrases, or lines). You can also add sound effects and music to help create desired moods.

Discuss It

Natural disasters occur in many places in the world and have negative effects on people and landscapes. Preparing for natural disasters can help us survive them and reduce their harmful effects.

Conduct a Discussion

Purpose

A discussion allows you to express your thinking about a topic while considering the views of others.

How to do it

- Decide on the role each person will play in the discussion.
- Develop a set of criteria to assess your group's discussion.
- Find out how much time you have for the discussion.
- Do not be satisfied until you have fully explored the questions you have been asked to discuss.

HINTS

When speaking and listening...

- Ask questions that make people think.
- Listen actively.
- Respect the ideas of others.
- Summarize ideas as you go.

TRY THIS

Discuss ideas about preparing for and surviving natural disasters.

The **leader** defines the task, keeps the group on task, and suggests new ways of looking at things.
The **reporter** presents the group's ideas to the class.
The **note maker** records ideas and clarifies the ideas with the group before recording.
The **supporter** provides positive feedback for each speaker, makes sure everyone gets a turn, and intercepts negative behaviour.
The **manager** gathers and summarizes materials the group will need, keeps track of time, and collects materials the group uses.

In a small group, discuss the following questions:

- What kinds of natural disasters are the most dangerous and why?
- What technologies can help people prepare for and reduce the impacts of a natural disaster (think about transportation, communication, engineering, and medical technologies)?

REFLECT ON SPEAKING

How can listening to the views of others help you to express your own opinions?

FROM THE GROUND UP

by Keltie Thomas

SOMETIMES THE FORCES OF NATURE ON Earth, make our planet quake, rumble, and blow its top. What's more, a strange atmosphere hovers over Earth. It is seen from outer space: fluffy white clouds of water vapour that swirl about the blue planet and eventually deliver what the weather's brewing.

Get Ready

- Preview the text. With a partner, list five things you notice about how this selection is presented. What does your list tell you about the author's purpose?

Strange BUT TRUE

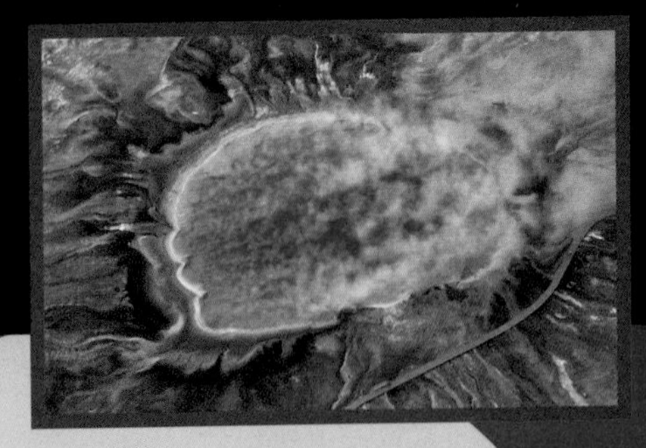

ONE-EYED PLANET

It looks like an eye! That's what you might think if you saw Grand Prismatic Spring from above. This hot spring is located in Yellowstone National Park in the United States. The spring supports heat-loving bacteria that may hold clues to how life first formed on Earth. Talk about having an eye on the world!

Earth Blows off Steam

On May 2, 2000, Steamboat, the world's tallest active geyser, went off for the first time in nine years. The gushing hot spring in Yellowstone National Park erupted with a major blast. The unpredictable old geyser shook the ground, roared, and fired a tall stream of boiling water into the air. And once it stopped gushing, the old geyser blew off a thunderous jet of steam about 152 m tall. Geysers pop up in spots where active or recently active volcanoes lie, such as Wyoming, Iceland, and New Zealand. Molten rock in these areas superheats groundwater, turning it into steam that builds into enormous pressure. Eventually, this steam and hot water get forced out of the ground and the geysers blow. What a rush, er, gush!

What rumbles, smells like rotten eggs, and flings mud? A mud volcano! Mud volcanoes are small cone-shaped mounds of mud and clay that Earth heaves up from below.

Earth Quakes in Its Boots

Earth quakes about a million times a year. Luckily, most of those earthquakes are too faint to notice. Phew! But every once in a while, Earth really quakes in its boots when parts of its crust, or outer shell, suddenly move. These shifts often occur along cracks, or faults, where two parts of the crust crunch together, push apart, or slide past each other. The sudden movement shakes all the surrounding rock, sending out shockwaves. Then, depending on how close you are to the quake's source, the ground beneath your feet may tremble. Windows may rattle, parked cars may sway back and forth, and buildings may topple over.

Ocean Cooks Up an Island

In November 1963, people all over the world had their eyes glued on the ocean off the coast of Iceland. The sea was on fire! Clouds of steam rose, rocks exploded out of the water, and black smoke climbed high into the sky. The fiery spectacle was the birth of an island as hot magma shot up from a volcano erupting on the sea floor. Over several months, the island took shape from steady lava flows. Today, Surtsey Island is a living laboratory for scientists studying how plants and animals come ashore and move in. The first puffin nests were found on the island in 2004.

It's Raining Frogs

The people of Naphilion, Greece, woke up to a strange sound one morning in 1981. To their surprise, it was the sound of small green frogs falling from the sky. And what was really surprising, was that the frogs were native to North Africa! How had the frogs become airborne to travel hundreds of kilometres away from their home? Some scientists suspect that waterspouts—tornado-like funnels of swirling air that form over water—may suck up creatures near the surface and carry them aloft. Then, wherever the waterspouts die out, they dump the creatures back to Earth.

Wave Freaks Out

Some waves turn into freak, or rogue, waves that have the size and power to wipe out a large ship. Sailors have been telling tales of freak waves half as wide as a football field and as tall as an office tower for hundreds of years. They say the monster water-walls rise straight up out of nowhere, followed by a deep trough like a hole in the sea. Until recently, many scientists thought rogue waves were just a myth. Now they've discovered that freak waves are the culprit in many ship sinkings, and are likely to occur where a swell crashes into a swirling current called an eddy.

React and Respond

1. Summarize the ideas presented in this selection using the headings "Atmospheric Forces" and "Internal Forces." Compare this to the information in *Dynamic Planet* on pages 14–15. What do you notice?
2. Identify how the author attempted to engage you as a reader. What words would you use to describe the author's voice?

MEDIA FILE

- Read like a news writer. What makes the stories in this selection "news-worthy"?
- Work with a small group. Role-play a TV news broadcast of one of the events. Before you create your broadcast, create a profile of your station's viewers. Make sure your news broadcast will catch and hold their attention.

Analyze News Media

We like to think that our news is "objective," free from point of view. Although most journalists try to present people and events in an unbiased way, all communication has a point of view. In the news reports below, various points of view are represented.

What techniques did the journalist use to attract my attention?

What values and points of view are represented in or omitted from this message?

How does the journalist want me to think or feel about the information? How do I know?

TRY THIS

Take a critical stance. Compare two news reports about a disaster from two different sources.

Compare News Reports

Look for similarities and differences.

- Identify the source of each report.
- What do you know about the audience it usually attracts?
- Record the headlines and opening sentences. What key words are used?
- Examine the points of view presented. Who is quoted? Who is left out?
- Note words that have emotional impact. Who or what do they describe? Are they positive or negative?

HINTS

When analyzing photographs, ask yourself...

- What is the photograph about?
- What do I already know about the topic of the photograph?
- What do I look at first in the photograph?
- What is the photographer trying to tell me or make me believe?

- Write a one-sentence summary of each article in your own words: "This reporter thinks that..."
- Share your analysis with two other students:

  What differences do you notice in the point of view presented in the two reports?

  Which report gives a more balanced view of the event?

REFLECT ON MEDIA

Explain how reading, writing, and discussing helped you make sense of news reports.

Excerpt from

AVALANCHE

by Paul Kropp

Get Ready

- Visualize. As you read this story, imagine that you are one of the characters. Would you react as he or she does in the story?

At 7:08 that morning, a dot of snow moved on the side of a mountain. The dot of snow moved just a few buried snowflakes around it. Those snowflakes jiggled and slid. Over them, a heavy layer of snow was waiting for that moment. It began to slide. The sliding was easy once it began. The snow was at a 40 degree angle. It was waiting for the moment when the first dot would move.

Five seconds later it was sliding fast. There was a roar as the snow slid down the mountain. It built up speed—faster and faster. Soon it would be going 100 km/hr, as fast as a car. It would weigh 100 tonnes. Anything in its path would be crushed.

On a nearby mountain there were two winter campers. The day before, they had seen some school kids come in on their snowshoes. They had watched them set up their tents and make a fire.

This morning they were awake early. "Crack of dawn," said Rick Marshall to his wife, Abby. They were actually up just before dawn. By seven, they were dressed and ready to go.

"What's the warning level?" Abby asked.

"Still *yellow*," Rick replied. *Natural avalanches unlikely. Human-triggered avalanches possible*, that's what it meant.

"Well, we should be good to go," replied his wife.

Then they heard the CRACK, though it was soon followed by a roar. Across from them, on another mountain, the snow was sliding.

"Oh no!" screamed Abby. "The kids!"

The kids were down below. They were in their camp, most of them still asleep in their tents. Only three kids were awake and outside when the snow let loose.

Mike Conroy had woken up early that day. His muscles hurt from snowshoeing the day before. His tent buddy snored. Wind made the tent rattle. Mike had a hard time sleeping and woke up in a bad mood just as the sun was rising.

Mike lay in his sleeping bag, in the cold. He thought about the trip, how it was half finished. They had done all they had planned. Now it was time for the group to turn around and head back.

It was supposed to "build character," this trip. *Whatever that means*, Mike thought to himself. He thought about Sid Grafton, snoring, and wondered if he should punch him to make him stop. He thought about the girls and stuck-up Brooke Ashton. He'd asked her out once and she'd turned him down cold. Now she was hooking up with Noah. *Noah!* Of all the guys in the school, he was the least likely. *What did that stuck-up girl see in Noah?* he thought. *Why was she so stupid that she didn't like me?*

Mike pulled on his jacket. He looked down at still-sleeping Sid and the avalanche beacon beside him. Mike shook his head. "You wuss," he said, mostly to himself.

Then he crawled through the tent flap and went outside. It was cold, very cold. He pulled himself up and walked to one side. Then he heard the crack…that became a roar.

Mike stood there, frozen, as the sheet of snow came down. He kept thinking it would stop farther up the hill. He kept thinking the snow could not reach him.

But in twenty seconds, it was there. The wall of snow hit Mike like a freight train, crushing his ribs. And then it buried him.

At six o'clock, Noah was dressed and ready. He was waiting for the first bit of sun. Then he stuck his head out the tent flap to see if the sun was up. Then he stared at his watch. Time seemed frozen—moving slowly minute by minute.

At 6:30, the sun peeked over a mountain. Noah was up in a flash. He grabbed his coat, his beacon and his shovel—ready to start the day. In fact, the most important part of the day was right now.

Outside it was cold—just at the freezing mark. The sliver of sun gave an orange light to the snow. To Noah, it seemed that the whole world was golden. There was no movement from any of the other tents. Most of the winter hikers were asleep, or staying in their sleeping bags to stay warm. But Noah was too excited to feel alone. He stamped his feet and tried to warm up. Where was she?

Then, Noah saw a movement in one of the tents. A flap pushed open and out came Brooke in her parka. She threw off the hood and smiled at Noah.

"Hey," she said.

"Hey," he replied, suddenly shy. They had spent the whole previous day together, but now he felt awkward. He didn't feel worthy of this girl.

"Cold," she said.

"Yeah," he agreed. And then he just blurted out, "You're beautiful. I mean, in this light, you are so beautiful."

"Oh, my hair…" she complained, but then stopped and looked into Noah's eyes.

At 7:08, Noah and Brooke heard the crack. They quickly looked up at the mountain to the north. Some snow had broken off and started to slide. The movement was slow at first, like a slow-motion film. Then the slide picked up speed. A roar of sound filled the valley.

Noah saw that the avalanche wasn't stopping. He had no words—there were no words. Instead, he stepped between Brooke and the sliding snow. He wanted his body to be a shield, to protect her—somehow, somehow.

It was Brooke who saw the wall of snow just before it hit them.

Rescuers

Abby Marshall was there first. She was a better skier than her husband, and made it down the mountain in minutes. At the same time, Rick Marshall was on the satellite phone.

"Avalanche!" screamed Rick Marshall into the phone. "Maybe twenty kids are buried. We need help—fast."

To Rick, the time on the phone was terrible. Each minute made a big difference. But the rescue centre needed a location. It took Rick a minute to find his GPS. It took him still more minutes to call the location through.

Down below him, the scene was a horror. A few orange tents peeked through the snow, but most were buried. It looked like

their anchors had held, so that gave them some hope. And the tents would give the kids some protection. But the Marshalls knew each minute made a big difference.

A person buried under snow has perhaps thirty minutes to live, if he is able to breathe, if he isn't bleeding. In an hour, anyone still buried would be dead.

When Rick got down the hill, his wife had already saved three kids. She used her shovel to break through the two tents she could see. Inside the tents, dazed and scared, were three kids. Tom, Mouse, and Boxcar were fast on their feet.

"Where's Noah?" Tom cried.

"No time," Rick shouted. "Grab shovels and dig! Anywhere you see anything!"

"I've got a beacon!" one kid shouted.

"Thank God," Abby said, running over to him.

The avalanche beacon gave them a chance. The closer the beacon got to a buried student, the louder it beeped. In Abby's hands, it led them from spot to spot.

Digging was not easy. The snow was almost like concrete—hard and heavy. The rescuers dug like madmen, but it seemed so slow.

They found people under the surface in ones and twos. In one spot they found Sid Grafton, Terry Morton, and Bones. In another

spot were Mrs. Falletta, Sarah, Rachel, G.G., and Tamara. Now they had half the boys, one teacher, and all the girls except for Brooke.

It was twenty minutes after the avalanche. But more help was coming. Two winter campers joined the search crew. Two park rangers came in on a snowmobile. Now there were six people with avalanche beacons, and eight were digging.

In the distance, there was the faint sound of a helicopter. More help was coming each minute, but would there be enough—in time?

Under the snow

The snow had hit Noah like an enormous wave. He was holding Brooke when the avalanche smashed into his back. There was a flash of pain. Then he was rolling, fighting, drowning.

It was like fighting against a tidal wave. Noah was rolled, pushed, smashed and finally buried. He had tried to hold onto Brooke. He had tried to protect her, but the falling wall of snow was too strong. The avalanche pulled Brooke from his arms; then, it took Noah down the mountain.

When the falling had stopped, Noah was just a crumpled, bent shape beneath the snow. His knees were at his elbows, his hands were at his face.

Around him it was dark and silent, like a tomb. No, not that dark, in truth. There was a little light that made its way through the white snow to Noah's eyes. He was breathing into his cupped hands. It was the breathing that told Noah he was alive.

Shock does strange things to a human being. It hides pain. It gives strength. It helps a person find the will to live.

Noah was in shock. Though he did not know it, his right leg was broken and two of his ribs were cracked. Though he could not know it, he was bleeding inside. If the bleeding did not stop, he would soon be dead.

Noah only knew that he was trapped by the snow. He tried to push with one leg, but there was too much pain. He tried to push with the other leg and the packed snow felt like concrete. He tried to twist, but the snow held him in its icy grip.

Air, he said to himself, *I need air!* He used his fingers to claw at the snow in front of his face. His breath had made that snow wet and just a bit soft. He slowly enlarged the small space in front of his face.

I can't be too far under the surface, he told himself.

Noah was right about that. If he were deep in the snow, he would have used up his little pocket of air by now. The fact that he could still breathe gave him hope. Air can move through two metres of snow—not much air, but enough to keep a person alive.

If I don't breathe too much, he thought. *If I don't panic...*

Panic is what kills you, he remembered. He had read that somewhere—if you can just keep your head straight, your chance of survival goes way up. Noah knew he had to control his thoughts. If he thought about being buried, he'd lose it. If he thought about being trapped in the snow, he'd start breathing too hard.

Noah began digging. He felt like a prisoner in jail, digging his way out, bit by tiny bit. Except that someone in jail had years to escape; Noah had less than an hour.

Someone will find me, he told himself. Noah's avalanche beacon was on. If it hadn't been crushed by the snow, it would tell them where he was. Surely it was only a matter of time till someone would come. But how much time?

After fifteen minutes, Noah's fingers became too weak to dig at the snow. The pain in his legs and sides kept jabbing at him. He could no longer feel his feet. He wondered if that's what frostbite was like. Perhaps a person just stopped feeling the dead flesh. Perhaps his feet would be the first to die.

Noah felt like he was going underwater. *How many more minutes?*, he wondered. *And what then? What happens after this life is over?* The idea of death felt like a warm bath. At least it would end this slow, dark torture...the slow oozing of his life into the snow.

Then Noah felt a sharp pain in his back, like he'd been jabbed. "Hey!" he shouted into the wet snow. The jabbing pain came back again, and then it stopped.

There was sound. Somewhere—over his head, around him—there was some crunching or digging or thumping. The sounds all seemed so strange, so confused.

Somehow, the snow in front of him was getting brighter. There was more light now, and it was easier to breathe. The sounds got louder, but now Noah could take a deep breath. The pain in his legs and his side grew worse, but something was happening. There were hands all around him, digging at the snow, scraping at the ice.

"Is he alive?" came a voice from above. Noah knew that voice from a life he'd had once. It was a voice from some time he remembered, from a time long ago.

Above him, Noah suddenly saw a blinding white sky and the shadow of a face. He could hear someone shouting—someone he knew.

"Hang on, Noah. You're going to make it," Tom cried. "You've got to make it!"

React and Respond

1. Outline the events of the story in a list, map, or timeline. Use your outline to help explain how the author builds suspense.
2. Work with a partner or a group to plan a TV movie for teens about the avalanche. Include ideas about your cast, how you would film the avalanche scene, and other features you could add.

COMPARE TEXTS

With a partner, make a chart. Compare the purpose of *Avalanche* and two other selections in the unit. Include the following in your chart:

- What type of text is it?
- Why was each selection written?
- How might each selection be used?
- What was the intended effect on the reader?

Discuss the similarities and differences. In your opinion, which selection deals with the topic of natural disasters most effectively? Why?

SHOW WHAT YOU KNOW

Create a Media Kit

You are going to work in a group to create a media kit about how to prepare for a natural disaster in your community.

A **media kit** is a collection of different information that a person or organization sends to media outlets (e.g., TV stations, newspapers) to get their message out.

Media Kit: How to Survive a Tornado

PRESS RELEASE

Emergency Preparedness Matters

The purpose of this kit is to provide you with the information you need to know to survive a tornado.

In this kit you will find a FAQ sheet that includes the questions Canadians ask most often about tornado safety. You find other information that will help you in the case of a torn…

DID YOU KNOW?

- The average speed of a tornado is 40 to 65 km/h. The safest thing you can do is look for a strong shelter of some kind and stay there until the tornado has passed.
- Tornadoes usually occur from April to September. Most tornadoes occur in June and July.
- Canada and the United States get the most tornadoes.

Media kit, student sample

Think about what you read, viewed, and discussed in this unit before you begin.

Topic	*Our community needs to be better prepared for a...*
Purpose	*Provide background material to media outlets to help get your message out.*
Audience	*Local or national media; TV, radio, newspapers, Web site*
Form	*Media kit*

PLAN YOUR MEDIA KIT

List the contents and decide who will produce each piece. For example, you might include...

- a cover letter or press release that identifies the issue and explains why it is important
- a collection of three to five visuals (e.g., photographs, graphs, symbols, video clip)
- a one or two page *Did You Know* or research backgrounder
- a *To Find out More* page (e.g., Web links, with a short description of the contents)

MORE IDEAS

- Choose other items for the kit (e.g., buttons, slogans, a poster, a link to a podcast).
- Create some or all of your materials as a video or podcast.

PRODUCE YOUR MEDIA KIT

Put your kit together. Work together to give feedback and revise the items in the kit. Then put them in a folder or box.

Exchange your kit with another group.

Give each other feedback about what catches your attention. Which parts would you use if you were in a newsroom?

LOOK FOR...

- newsworthy content
- convincing explanation of the importance of the issue
- accurate information
- clear writing and organization
- items that are quick and easy to use

REFLECT

- What aspects of your media kit are you most satisfied with?
- What does your media kit show about your understanding of purpose and audience? What else does it show about your learning?

Develop Your Portfolio

- Choose two or three pieces of work that show your learning.
- Be prepared to share them with your teacher, family and friends.

Acknowledgements

Permission to reprint copyrighted material is gratefully acknowledged. Every effort has been made to trace ownership of all copyrighted material and to secure permission from copyright holders. In the event of any questions arising as to the use of any material, we will be pleased to make the necessary corrections in future printings.

Photographs

Cover G Brad Lewis/Riser/Getty Images; **1** G Brad Lewis/Riser/Getty Images; **6-7** Alberto Garcia/Corbis Canada; **8** Amblin/Universal/Warners/ The Kobal Collection; **9** top 20th Century Fox/The Kobal Collection; bottom 20th Century Fox/The Kobal Collection; **10** top Warner Bros/The Kobal Collection; bottom Universal/The Kobal Collection/Glass, Ben; Universal/The Kobal Collection; **11** Universal/The Kobal Collection; **12-13** left to right Corbis Canada; G Brad Lewis/Riser/Getty Images; John Sevigny/epa/ Corbis Canada; Alberto Garcia/Corbis Canada; JUPITERIMAGES/Brand X/Alamy; **14** Photodisc; **16** Don Farrall/Photodisc/Getty Images; **17** bottom right Reuters/Corbis Canada; **18** AP Photos; **19** Daniel Leclair/Reuters/Corbis Canada; **20** Klaus Nigge/ National Geographic Image Collection; **21** left AP Photos; **22** AMATEUR VIDEO/Reuters /Landov; **23** Getty Images; **24-25** Art Wolfe/Riser/Getty Images; **25** CHAIWAT SUBPRASOM/Reuters/Corbis Canada; **26-27** Anuruddha Lokuhapuarachchi/ Reuters/Corbis Canada; **26** bottom Penny Boyd/Alamy; **28-29** Reuters/ Corbis Canada; **30-31** AP Photos; **32** centre ABC Ajansi/Corbis Sygma; inset Ekberzade Bikem/Corbis Sygma; **33** Reuters/Corbis Canada; **34-35** Mark Muench/Stone/ Getty Images; inset Jacques Langevin/ Corbis Sygma; **36** top left Johannes Kroemer/ Photonica/Getty Images; centre right Lowell Georgia/ Corbis Canada; bottom left Jeremy Walker/ Science Photo Library; **36-37** bottom Juniors Bildarchiv/Alamy; **37** top David Samuel Robbins/Corbis Canada; **38-39** left to right Corbis Canada; G Brad Lewis/Riser/Getty Images; John Sevigny/epa/Corbis Canada; Alberto Garcia/Corbis Canada; JUPITERIMAGES/Brand X/ Alamy; **38** CP Photo/ Montreal La Presse-Martin Chamberland; **40-41** Steven Puetzer/Nonstock/ firstlight.ca; **42-43** left to right Corbis Canada; G Brad Lewis/Riser/Getty Images; John Sevigny/epa/Corbis Canada; Alberto Garcia/Corbis Canada; JUPITERIMAGES/Brand X/Alamy; **44** Robert Berger / Imagestate; **45** Jupiter Images; top right NPS Photo; **46-47** background Mark Downey/ Photodisc/ Getty Images; **46** top Photodisc/ firstlight.ca; centre Wesley Bocxe/Photo Researchers, Inc.; bottom Elvele Images/Alamy; **47** left Warren Bolster/Stone/ Getty Images; right Keren Su/Digital Vision/Getty Images; **47-48** left to right Corbis Canada; G Brad Lewis/Riser/ Getty Images; John Sevigny/ epa/Corbis Canada; Alberto Garcia/Corbis Canada; JUPITERIMAGES/ Brand X/Alamy; **48** left REUTERS/ Brian Snyder /Landov; top right REUTERS/Rick Wilking/Landov; bottom right DAVID CARSON/UPI/ Landov; **58-59** top Alberto Garcia/Corbis Canada.

Illustrations

12-13, **15**, **17**, **19**, **23** Christiane Beauregard; **17**, **18**, **21**, **25**, **29**, **32-33**, **35** Tad Majewski; **43** Tina Holdcroft; **50-56** Paul Rivoche; **58** Rose Zgodzinski.

Text

"Nature's Warning System" from *Tsunami*: TAJ Books © 2005; "Learning from Tragedy: Izmit 1999" excerpt reprinted from *The Atlas of Natural Disasters* by Jeff Groman: Z Publishing Ltd. © 2001 by permission; "Bend It & Pad It" adapted with the permission of Margaret K. McElderry Books, an Imprint of Simon & Schuster Children's Publishing Division from *Earthquake Games* by Matthys Levy and Mario Salvadori. Text copyright © 1997 Matthys Levy and Mario Salvadori; "Avalanche Alert!" (adapted from original titles "Landslides and Avalanches" and "Avalanche") from *Natural Disasters*, by Claire Watts and Trevor Day, published by DK Publishing Inc.: Eye Witness Books, New York, NY, © 2006 and from *Hurricane and Tornado*, by Jack Challoner, published by DK Publishing Inc.: Eye Witness Books, New York, NY, © 2004; "Natural Disasters" from *Footprints on the Roof: Poems about the Earth* by Marilyn Singer, copyright © 2002 by Marilyn Singer. Used by permission of Alfred A. Knopf, an imprint of Random House Children's Books, a division of Random House, Inc.; "From the Ground Up" from *Shake "n" Quake Planet: Planet Earth News Presents Nature Shockers* by Keltie Thomas and illustrated by Greg Hall, Maple Tree Press Inc. © 2005; "Avalanche" excerpt from *Avalanche* by Paul Kropp: High Interest Publishing an imprint of Chestnut Publishing © 2005.